CALIFORNIA

A Vanished
Cuisine—Rediscovered

CALIFORNIA

MISSION COOKERY

A Vanished
Cuisine—Rediscovered

by Mark Preston

Border Books

P.O. Box 80780
Albuquerque, NM 87198
(505) 266-8322

Edited by Dave DeWitt
Book Design by Lois Bergthold and Deborah Beldring

Printed in the United States of America

ISBN 0-9623865-5-3

How to Order:
Quantity discounts are available from Border Books, P.O. Box 80780, Albuquerque,
New Mexico 87198; telephone (505) 266-8322. On your letterhead include informa-
tion concerning the intended use of the books and the number of books you wish to
purchase.

DEDICATION

To my mother, Edyth Preston, who gave me my love of cooking and food, and to all the early Californio cookbook writers and compilers who knew good food and helped to preserve the past, I gratefully dedicate this book.

ACKNOWLEDGMENTS

No writer could have had more honest help than I received on this project. I wish to thank many people for inspiration.

To Julia Child and Diana Kennedy for the inspiration to grow, culinarily— and especially to Mrs. Kennedy for her critiques of some of my writing.

To Ronald and Patricia Guentzler, the finest cooks I have ever had the pleasure to dine with. Thank you for more than any feelings I could ever put into words.

To Lou Moench, owner of Your Father's Office in Santa Monica, California. As strange a name as it sounds, Father's serves thirty or so hand-crafted beers. Lou was an inspiration of the need for a return to good taste.

To Bob Brewer, international brewery representative of the Anchor Brewing Company and to his boss, Fritz Maytag, who single-handedly saved the only beer brewed in America in a unique style—for their words (and deeds) of encouragement about food and drink.

To Larry Rizzo and Wayne Fox for helping to make my research possible.

To Leo Nuñez at the Bandido Restaurant for help with translations.

To Brian Schottlaender for hiring me at the Shack Annex Project.

To my editor, Dave DeWitt, for forcing me to do more on this project and then taking his valuable time to assist.

To Robert Spiegel for taking a chance that my writing is unique, and to Lois Bergthold, the book's graphic designer, for listening to my long-winded suggestions about how a book should look and feel.

Also thanks to Daniel Strehl of the Los Angeles Public Library for upfront and ongoing support of this work, including personal loans of rare manuscripts.

And to John Vittal, inter-library loan specialist at the Albuquerque Public Library, as well as Julia Clark, head librarian of the Lomas-Tramway branch library for her generosity of time.

Grateful appreciation is given to the following for permission to use certain materials:

The Arthur H. Clark Company of Spokane Washington for *Early California Hospitality* by Ana Bégué de Packman.

Dan Strehl of the Los Angeles Public Library for use of his translations of Encarnación Pinedo's *El Cocinero Español*.

CONTENTS

INTRODUCTION

In 1987, I was fortunate enough to be employed as a book cataloguer by the State of California for the University of California library system. The University Libraries had, for twenty years prior to the term of my employment, set aside books that were either gifts or purchases.

First, the gifts. Irene Greene Dwen Pace, wife of Admiral Pace, had been a book collector, and the Pace Library ended up in library system as a bequest from her. I think that her children probably did not want to keep such a large number of books, and the bequest was, for them, a relief. Her collection alone consisted of 10,000 or more books, and of those, about 2,000 were cookbooks. Additionally, there were simple bequests from others of just fifty or a hundred books. These donors were sensible souls who knew that to preserve the past was to preserve mankind's cultural heritage.

The purchases consisted of The Regents of the University of California buying out whole libraries of European aristocracy. There were, among others, Phillippe Napoleon's books—or at least some of them. Another form of purchase was that of bookstores that had gone out of business. Sometimes these purchases comprised tens of thousands of books.

The total quantity of books to be catalogued was around 138,000, and I personally inspected each one. And while I didn't have time enough to do more than briefly scan each one, just seeing the collected thoughts of mankind was a unique and influential experience.

The books I devoted my time to were published between the sixteenth century to the twentieth century. I held books in my hands as old as about 1500 or as new as the 1960s. By the 1970s, the Library System had installed powerful computers, and the work of cataloguing had become computerized.

Now, ordinarily, 100,000 books of every possible subject would be something of a bore, as anybody who has ever seen the stacks at a major university library will attest to. However, these books had been selected by their former owners with an eye towards what in the book trade is called bibliophilia. I prefer the word bibliomania because it has more whimsy. These collections, consisted of, on the whole, more fine printing, rare or first editions, and unusual bindery work than any other 100,000 odd books, just sitting on shelves, anywhere.

My work consisted of reviewing each book to meet the requirements for inclusion in the National Union Database computer system. This database is a record of all the books held in more than 35,000 libraries worldwide. The total number of books is approximately thirty-five million. During my employment with the University, I processed about 27,000 books. While only a few of those were cookbooks, they were some of the most interesting works.

As the cookbooks started to come through the cataloguing process, I was able to keep a record of many of them. One in particular I remember was a cookbook for a Low-Cholesterol diet from the 1950s—a book well ahead of it's time. How I came across *California Mexican-Spanish Cook Book* is another tale.

By reading more of the cookbooks than perhaps I should have, I came to have a sense of the history of cooking. When I was at the computer terminal one day, I chanced to search the database for *Mexican Cooking*. This showed the existence of a previously unseen work from a lady with a somewhat unusual name: Mrs. Bertha Hafner-Ginger. At least, that is the name given on the computer screen. After some trouble, I obtained a copy of her work. Her words, thoughts, ideas, and recipes were just as fresh the day I first read them as the day they were printed. And as I read her recipes, I was transported back to turn-of-the-century California—back to the "Land of Sunshine," a golden state of fiestas and rodeos lasting for many days. It was a time when there was clean air, clear water, orange groves, and cattle grazing on a thousand hills. It was a time of *charros*, Mexican gentleman farmers in the mold of Thomas Jefferson and flashing dark-eyed senoritas with roses held between their teeth as they danced the *jota*.

From these California images emerged Bertha and her cookbook. Bertha's recipes stood the test of time better than any other cookbook that I have ever seen on any cuisine. She had to self-publish the book, and only a few copies found their way into the hands of librarians. In fact, there are only four or five copies of her work known to exist. Two are held in Southern California, one in Pennsylvania, and one at the Library of Congress.

On a more personal note, my love of cooking and eating arises from the fact that my mother ran a tearoom when I was a small boy, so I grew up on the finest cooking imaginable. My mother, Edyth Preston, was of French extraction, and her mother, Louise Toussaint, had taught her to cook in the French style.

Interestingly, my mother Edyth was cooking French cuisine contemporaneously with Julia Child. Her tearoom served about fifty women a luncheon about three or four times a week. My father and I were served whatever was on the menu that day—from a simple roast beef or roast chicken to often something fancier. I remember the wonder of the fresh food. The sliced fresh tomatoes, served with just a pinch of salt, came directly from the garden in back of the barn and would be still warm from the vine. Milk came from the neighbors' cows, and pork sausage was made from a suckling pig. A peach stolen off the neighbor's tree would be ripe in the summer's heat. This is the food I grew up eating. It spoiled me for the rest of my life, and that's why Bertha's book made my mouth water, again.

Inspired by Bertha's *California Mexican-Spanish Cook Book*, I searched for other obscure books that captured the spirit of the original California Mission cookery. This book is the result of that research.

San Gabriel Archangel Mission, near Los Angeles
Paul Elder Publishing, Circa 1911

CHAPTER 1

Californio Cuisine

T his cookbook presents recipes from a lost cuisine. Why and how an entire style of cooking would vanish is, ultimately, only the subject of guesswork. Cookery has its trends, some fads, and not a few follies. Trends may come and go, but seldom has an entire school of cooking so thoroughly vanished as that of the nineteenth century Californios. Their cuisine was, from the time of the early settlements to the beginning of the twentieth century, as earthy, fresh, light, and bright as any European or Asian cookery. Californio cuisine was a tale told from *tierra, cielo, y mar*—earth, sky, and sea.

A brief note on the use of the adjective "Mexican" is in order. Social custom, political change, and local usage make finding *the* correct term for the original California cuisine (such as "Mexican food") almost an impossibility. Mexican food, as the term is used here, is applied only to those dishes and plates as prepared by the original Mexicans of California. Before they became Mexicans, they were Spanish Colonialists who lived in California. They preferred to call themselves *Californios*. Anglos, at the turn of the century, called them Spaniards. Here, the term "Californio" is preferred for the earliest form of California cuisine and is used throughout this work.

It is historic fact that after 1849, California became a culinary melting pot. Take one part Native Indian, add some Spanish zest, throw in a few Sourdough Gold Rushers, and the melting pot had begun. Before 1849, California was almost an island on the land. Separated from Spanish Colonial rule in Mexico City by thousands upon thousands of miles, governmental edicts did not reach the Californias until years after their enactment. Even during the Mexican regime, communication between Mexico City and Monterey or Los Angeles was still so slow that the pioneers did not hear the news of Mexican Independence from Spain until a year went by. During the Americanization period (approximately 1847 to the coming of the railroad) any news, mail, and legal matters still moved at a pace more feudal than the rest of the world in the mid-nineteenth century. The telegraph did not even reach Los Angeles until 1860.

America developed, at first, colony by colony. The English settled New England, and Scandinavians settled in Wisconsin and Minnesota. St. Louis, Missouri still has an enclave known as the South Side Dutch—they are Germans who emigrated early in the nineteenth century. Chicago has the largest Polish community outside Warsaw. One important fact is that all of these cultures brought their cuisines with them, and they kept those cuisines alive to this day. These ethnic neighborhoods have continued to flourish despite intermarriage, upward mobility, and the social changes and pressures of the twentieth century.

This pattern does not exist with the original California cuisine, that gem of cooking practiced by the Californios. *That* California cuisine incorporated the abundance of native produce and meats. It was born in the era of the *conquistador*. It thrived and grew during the changing forms of government, from Spanish Colonial to Mexican and then from Mexican to Californian and lastly to American. It thrived after the dissolution of the vast *ranchos* and the coming

2

of the Anglos and the railroad.

Then, it just vanished. Between 1915 and 1940, fewer than a dozen cookbooks were written on how to cook *en estilo Californio* or on how to cook "Mexican" food. Thus, the original California cuisine, as practiced in the Missions and on the *ranchos* and *haciendas* of old, disappeared. Yet, during its heyday, it swept the nation, leaving only a few words of its grand style behind: *tamales, chile con carne, barbacoa*, and *calabash*.

California cuisine began with the indigenous peoples of California. The Native Americans utilized such staples as nuts, berries, fruits, fish, and game, and a type of nut gruel was basic to their diet. Their cooking techniques were primitive but effective, and they steamed or boiled foods in woven baskets by placing hot stones in them.

With the coming of the Spanish—first the missionaries, then the soldiers, and lastly the pioneers—the lot of the Native Americans began to change rapidly. The Padres were disturbed by the impoverished appearance of the Native Americans and forced them to wear clothes, and to stop bathing. The Padres developed a cuisine to feed them, in order to turn them into farmers.

Some foodstuffs, such as vegetables, nuts, fruits, and seafood were adapted directly into the Spanish style of cooking that the missionaries brought with them, along with Old World foods such as beef and pork. The also brought New World foods directly from Mexico City: beans, corn, tomatoes, chiles, and avocados. The Mission kitchens would combine the Old and New World elements and prepare large feasts for the *fiesta* days. At the height of its glory, the Mission San Gabriel reported killing 100 head of cattle each Saturday for the 500 inhabitants. The Native Americans from all the *rancherias* in the neighborhood would show up for the feasts, which were the beginnings of a new, dynamic cuisine.

The growth of California, prior to the coming of the American, set a table of native ingredients cooked in a Spanish manner. From the Missions, this style of cooking was transferred to the outlying *ranchos*, which operated like medieval fiefdoms. The serfs (Native Americans) farmed the lands and gave their produce to the barons (Dons of California). The barons and their families did very little work and considered themselves to be the aristocracy.

However, they were the intrepid pioneers who had the vision of a new life in California. They had been awarded land grants as a reward for serving the Crown, mostly as soliders. The Dons created the vast *ranchos* and their attendant *vaqueros* (cowboys), *campasenos* (agricultural laborers), and, of course, the large kitchen staffs which had to feed everyone. On the California *ranchos*, the produce grew bigger and better because of a 360 day-per-year growing season. Cattle roamed freely and fed on grasses that grew higher than a full grown man.

But this idyllic life was not to last. Between about 1770 and 1870, the Missions and *ranchos* came into existence, flourished, and then disappeared forever. The Mission lands were first taken by the Dons and then, later by the Americans.

The first great waves of immigration to California started with the '49ers and continued with the railroad price wars of the late 1880s. Ticket prices between Kansas City and Los Angeles plunged. Easterners and Midwesterners streamed into California. They built homes and hired servants. Sometimes, these servants were not busy with their employers' work. Perhaps on a sunny Saturday afternoon, the servants would prepare wonderful dishes for themselves—lunches whose ingredients would make the mansion redolent with the aroma that came from their native cooking. The aroma, wafting through the house, would tantalize the Anglo family. The husband probably asked the wife to find out what was cooking. The wife would return with the answer—dishes with strange names like *tacos, enchiladas, tortas, chiles rellenos,* or *guisados de carne.* Probably, the husband commented that he would like to try such a dish, and from then on, Californio food started finding its way onto Anglo tables.

If some of the servants spoke a little English, or the lady of the house learned a little Spanish, the ethnic luncheon would be ordered and the whole household would feast upon it. Neighbors and friends would be feted with the exotic dishes. Perhaps the children of the upstairs would play with the *niños* of the downstairs. After a strenuous game of hide and go-seek, the children were hungry. The *madre del niños* would create some *antojitos,* or appetizers of *tacos* or *quesadillas.* The flavors of oregano, epazote, chile, avocado, and garlic would soon cease to be foreign.

However, when the vast *ranchos* were divided up among heirs and reduced to mere garden plots, and when urban development and tourism took over, Californio Cuisine slowly disappeared. By 1888, the time of the second great wave of immigration, the era of homes with servants declined. There just weren't enough hired hands to go around. Los Angeles had grown from 4,000 people in the 1860s to 80,000 in the 1880s. San Francisco had a population of more than 150,000 in the 1860s, and its population growth continued to outpace Southern California for decades to come.

As the population grew, so did creativity and invention. Nineteenth century America was the birthplace of science in service to humanity. Tinned, packaged, and processed foods were the pinnacle of achievement in that age of invention. With the addition of piped gas to homes, the science of modern cookery had begun. This, coupled with the abundance of California foods shipped from railheads in Los Angeles to the American people, launched the demand for name brands. With the development of the tinned can, modern preservatives and the railroad transportation of citrus—especially the orange and lemon—California became synonymous with the word "fresh."

My grandfather, who lived in St. Louis, Missouri, told of receiving a gift at Christmas (about 1882) of a fresh California orange and a five dollar goldpiece. The first shipment of California oranges was in 1877. The trend toward national brands began at the turn of the century. For the next fifty years,

4

Americans were slowly exposed to the name brand. At first, this was a definite improvement over the lack of fruits, vegetables, and meats in the winter. Housewives learned that to make soup, all one had to do was open a can. A ham could be had with the turning of a key. Wholesomeness could be assured, seals didn't burst, and the food didn't spoil. It was a healthier America. In some ways, it was even a more culinary diverse America.

This trend toward canned, national brands was not to last, at least for the sophisticated palate. One reason it didn't last was that the canned, highly processed food was bland, and grandmothers could remember what really fresh food tasted like. Those fresh memories were based on the availability of locally-grown produce, brought to the market from only a short distance. With the mass urbanization of America from mid-century onward, farms near the cities gave way to what are now suburbs. The result was a decline in the sophistication of cooking in large cities. This trend was not reversed until magazines such as *Gourmet* started re-educating the American people.

By the 1920s, Californio cuisine was only a memory. What were people eating then? The influx of Easterners brought with them the "American" table. It would be described by Encarnacion Pinedo in her cookbook, *El Cocinera Español*, as follows: "The [Anglo] food and style of seasoning is the most insipid and tasteless as can be imagined."

The days of culinary sunshine were covered with clouds, and for a while, Californio cuisine was on the eclipse. That would all change very shortly in a period of remembrance. First, in southern California, there was a Mission Revival Period, followed a decade or two later throughout California by the Spanish Colonial Revival. Spurred by tourism turning into immigration, the citrus industry, cheap land, and the permanent establishment of the American government in what had been formerly Mexican territory, the people chose to look back at previous century fondly.

A classmate of President Teddy Roosevelt, Charles Lummis, founded The Landmark's Club. The Club's sole purpose was the preservation and recording of California's past glory. Had it not been for Lummis' efforts, many of today's Missions would have become bumps of mud in the baking sun. He also founded Los Angeles' Southwest Museum, dedicated to California's cultural heritage.

While Lummis and his Landmark's Club were gathering scraps of California culture to give authenticity to the Mission and Spanish Revivals, another form of culture was being preserved as well. How the *culinary* heritage was preserved is a strange tale indeed. It was captured by a school marm named Bertha Ginger. She taught tenth grade mathematics in the Compton School District. She was married twice, so she was also known as Mrs. Bertha Haffner-Ginger and later as Mrs. Bertha Palmer. In the early part of the twentieth century, she earned approximately $1000 per year—good money for that time. Yet, between husbands, money was tight. To supplement her income, she started teaching classes in what she called "California Mexican-Spanish" cooking.

5

Bertha found it difficult to pinpoint whether a Californian was Mexican, Spanish, or Californian, so she confusingly lumped all the terms together in the title of her self-published book, *California Mexican-Spanish Cook Book*.

Bertha developed a collection of gourmet recipes unique to Californio-style cooking, and she is the only one who preserved the cuisine in its totality. She is the first author of a book about the *original* California cuisine in the English language.

Prior to Bertha's self-published effort, there were charitable cookbooks which contained what they called "Spanish Sections." In these sections would be endless variations on *enchiladas* or *chile con carne*. There were other cookbooks published by the small, local newspaper of the time, *The Los Angeles Times*. It put out an annual series of cookbooks which contained *Californio* recipes. They were only slightly better recipes than those in the charitable fundraiser cookbooks. Lastly, there was another cookbook entitled *101 Mexican Dishes*, by May E. Southworth, published by Paul Elder in San Francisco in 1906, containing some *Californio* recipes. Yet none of these books approached Bertha's cookery for authenticity, subtlety, freshness, finesse, versatility, and simplicity. Her cookery is truly a unheralded landmark in the annals of California cookery. Many noted authors, ethnogastronomers, and bibliographers have somehow missed Bertha's work, originally published in 1914.

The term "California Cuisine" is not a recent phenomenon. As early as the 1940s, Helen Evans Brown, in her *California Cooks* recipe book used the phrase "California Cuisine." Californians, due largely to the Gold Rushers, came from everywhere. With them came their favorite foods. In the Land of Sunshine, it all blended harmoniously together into a delightful medley of dishes. Californians were using many foodstuffs long before the rest of the nation; for example, they served radicchio, guavas, avocados, and mangoes.

Rather than a unique cuisine *per se*, current California cuisine is a return to locally available, fresh ingredients. It is most often ingredients of the Americas, cooked with French or Italian influences. *But, it should be simple cooking*. Americans are by nature closer to the frying pan than to haute cuisine, to paraphrase Raymond Sokolov in his book, *Fading Feast*.

During the last thirty or so years, California cuisine, as it has become known, is largely a result of a negative reaction to the national brands of food products from the 1960s. It is also a reaction against the use of chemicals in all aspects of food production. It was during the 1960s that the local brand sputtered out of existence. Maybe this occurred because of large-scale production of national brands or because the children of the founders of the locally-made products found other work more interesting.

California cuisine is an avoidance of the hamburgerization and pizzafication of our culinary heritage. While more foodstuffs are available than ever before, genetically-engineered tomatoes still taste like cardboard. Statistically, America shifted dramatically from an agrarian society to an urban society in only twenty years' time. In the 1950s, fifteen percent of the population were farmers, but by the 1980s, that number had shrunk to less than two percent. From the 1950s onward, it became difficult in this country to obtain fresh, locally produced ingredients that were not either overprocessed or chemically altered.

California Cuisine currently blends several ethnic styles of cooking into something more unique than what came immediately before it. The foodstuffs that the Americas gave to this wonderful cuisine are: beans, chiles, turkey, corn, potatoes, tomatoes, avocados, and cocoa.

If California cuisine has a theme, it is that of fresh foods. If it has a story, it is that of simple preparation. If it has a message, it is that of the grill. It is the idea that food should speak from the plate. It doesn't matter whether the vegetables or the meats or both are grilled. In this, California cuisine has become very eclectic in recent years, offering, for example, Mexican Chicken with Raisins and Almonds. Here, in this recipe, in addition to the chicken, are chorizo sausage, serrano chiles, and lime juice—common enough ingredients for anywhere in Mexico. Yet, the addition of raisins and almonds makes the dish typical of California Cuisine.

As America now approaches another *fin de siecle*, California can look back on the previous century just as fondly. When Californio food first became popular in America, cooks across the land had to use canned or dried or otherwise processed ingredients for *that authentic taste*. What were tinned, or preserved, or processed foods in that era, are now available fresh in almost every market across America. Avocados, fresh chiles, squash, and cilantro are only a few of the items with which one can prepare authentic and original Californio cookery. The recipes in this book can be prepared as the Californios cooked them, garden fresh and with all the flavors speaking individually; yet, they are in harmony and speaking with all the subtle nuances that gourmet chefs want when their guests or families dine.

About the Recipes

I searched many early cookbooks for the original Californio Mission recipes, and as I assembled them for this book, I realized that I did not want to create another variation on the basic "Mexican" cookbook. Rather, I wanted the recipes to stand by themselves for the experienced cook. So, as much as possible, I have retained the actual words and form of the recipes because their rhythms of the kitchen are the cook's delight. The only changes were to correct spelling, or to clarify when needed and to give a list of ingredients first. It should be noted that the form of the recipes is not nearly as sophisticated as those in modern cookbooks, but they can be followed easily.

The earliest cookbooks that gave Californio-style recipes were written at a time when some of the true ingredients were unavailable. Bertha Ginger, for example, was forced to omit or substitute necessary ingredients, and she did so without comment. For example, she would sometimes specify parsley when cilantro was the requisite item. I have made such changes.

A number of recipes specify a sauce or salad dressing by number; for example, there is: "Chile Sauce No. 1." Bertha didn't always specify (or forgot) the number and called for either a red or green sauce. I have fixed this problem, so use the numbered sauces where they are called for.

The spelling and phrasing of the turn-of-the century cooks was not always precise, and their Spanish was not always perfect. I have left the recipe titles in their original form when possible. Sometimes chiles are chile peppers, but sometimes they are just called peppers. Sweet peppers are now called bell peppers. The word "pepper" alone always refers *Piper nigrum*, or black pepper. "Chile" or "Chile Pepper" means a Capsicum.

Chiles and Preparing Them

The chiles that are used most frequently in these recipes are commonly known as New Mexican in the United States. In California and other places, the produce industry often calls them Anaheim chiles. Technically speaking, an Anaheim chile is a variety of the New Mexican pod type that is adapted to California. Look for chiles that are about six inches long, have a tapered end, and are about one inch wide at the stem end. Other chiles that are used in the recipes are specified by variety, such as serrano, piquin, bell, and so on. Wherever serranos are called for, jalapeños will substitute, but the flavor will be slightly different.

Bertha Ginger's recipes, with their use of chile pulp, show their authenticity because a later age preferred powdered chiles. In old California, fresh chiles, whether red or green, were prepared *asada*, or grilled over coals to separate the skin from the meat of the chile. The chiles were turned frequently to prevent the burning of the skin, and the grilling mellowed the taste of the chiles and added a nuance of smoke.

The same technique is used today with a charcoal grill. If the skin burns too much, it will impart a bitter flavor to the chiles. A variation is to dip the chiles in boiling water to scald; or to turn them over on a griddle, pressing with a spatula; or even to deep fry them. In New Mexico, chiles are placed in cylindrical roasters that resemble fifty-five gallon drums. The exterior surface of the roaster is wire mesh. Propane jets produce the fire and are aimed into the roaster, and it is turned quickly for several minutes. The fragrance released from the roasting chiles is heavenly. Chiles can also be held over stovetop burners and grilled. Get them good and hot and don't let the skin burn too much. Place the chiles in a plastic bag for twenty minutes, and the skins will come off easily.

To prepare chile pulp, a food mill works well, but a food processor, while faster, does not give quite the same consistency. Unless otherwise stated, when cooking with chiles, use the seed, veins, and chile meat altogether. All pulps should be the consistency of pureed mashed potatoes. The following procedure for making pulp can be substituted for the directions in some of the individual recipes.

8

"Prepared" dried chiles are those that are soaked or simmered in hot water until they are limp. Split them open with a knife, and, using the back of a spoon or a vegetable peeler, scrape the pulp out and discard the skin, seeds, and stem.

The dry roasting of breadcrumbs, chiles, seeds, and herbs is done by heating a cast iron skillet or other heavy pot over low heat, adding what needs warming and removing them when the color changes or when the aroma rises from the skillet. This technique requires practice. Cumin take a little longer than oregano to finish. Therefore, to avoid scorching the oregano, the ingredients must constantly be stirred. Add the cumin before the oregano—timing is critical, so be careful!

All the recipes have been written to give the ingredients list first. For convenience, a description of the ingredient is also given. For example: 1 Chicken, cut up for frying, or ½ Tsp. Parsley, minced.

CHAPTER 2

Sauces, Relishes

&

Pickles

Sauce No. 1

RED CHILE SAUCE
for Enchiladas or Tamales, etc.

12 Dried Red Chiles
½ C. Lard or Olive Oil
1 T. Flour
Salt to taste

Toast the chiles. Split red chile pepper, remove all seeds and veins, soak for several hours in water, pour off, pour on boiling water, pour off and repeat the process again, with the last water just covering the peppers when pressed down. Mash in this water and press the chiles through a sieve to make red chile pulp. Melt the lard, add 1 heaping T. flour, brown, and add 3 C. red chile pulp, salt to taste, cook very slowly, for 30 minutes. Olive oil is a pleasant substitute for lard. In any event, the flour is nothing but a thickener.

Variation: Add white onion, garlic, cilantro, and oregano, quantities given below in Prepared Spanish Sauce.

Sauce No. 2

GREEN CHILE SAUCE
for Enchiladas or Tamales, etc.

This sauce was eaten on Huevos Rancheros on nippy mornings in the San Francisco Bay Area.

12 Green Chiles
¼ C. Lard or Olive Oil
2 T. Flour
1 Tsp. Salt

Split, remove seeds and veins from green chiles and boil in a little hot water till tender; mash, press through sieve to make pulp. Melt ¼ C. lard, add 2 T. flour, 1 Tsp. salt, brown just a little, add 3 C. green pulp, and cook slowly for 30 minutes.

Salsa Preparada
PREPARED SPANISH SAUCE

6 Red Chiles
6 Green Chiles
3 Red Bell Peppers
3 Green Bell Peppers
½ C. Olive Oil
½ White Onion, chopped
½ Cup Cilantro, chopped
3 Cloves Garlic, mashed
1 T. Oregano
2 C. Raw Tomatoes, chopped
6 Whole Cloves, ground
Salt

Take equal parts red and green chile peppers, same amount red and green bell peppers, split, remove seeds from all, soak in water, drain, add enough water to barely cover, boil till tender, mash in water, press through sieve to make pulp. Heat ½ C. olive oil, fry in it onion, cilantro, three garlic cloves, T. oregano, raw tomatoes, six cloves, 2 C. of the pepper pulp, salt to taste. Cook, strain, and reheat. Bottle larger quantities. A very fine sauce.

SPRINGTIME FOR L.A.

Émile C. Ortega opened the first chile canning plant in 1898. His chiles were roasted over hot coals and canned and shipped all over the United States. Ortega was the sheriff of Ventura County for a while but found chile canning more profitable. He had a daughter named Trinidad. She was the sweetheart of Lt. Edward Ord, the first American mapmaker of Colonial California. The city fathers had him lay out streets and give them names. Today's Spring Street, in downtown Los Angeles, was originally named Primavera, Spanish for springtime, in honor of Trinidad's nickname.

Mojo Criollo
COUNTRY MOJO

Mojo, the adjective from the verb *mojar*, means moistened. Process the mojo recipes so as to let the natural juices of the ingredients moisten the mixtures.

6 Oz. Parsley
6 Oz. Onions
Salt

Equal parts of both, chopped in the food processor but not to a purée. Add the salt to taste. Serve in a small molcajete or pretty bowl. Spread over fried or broiled meats.

Mojo de Ajo
GARLIC MOJO

½ C. Garlic, made into a paste
2 T. Olive Oil

Use a *molcajete* or food processor to process the garlic into a paste, then drop it into the hot oil. Immediately lower the heat, stir constantly to prevent burning, until thoroughly heated. Add some salt to taste. Good with any barbecued meat, but especially pork.

Salsa Español
SPANISH CATSUP

½ Gal. Green Cucumbers
½ Gal. Cabbage
12 Onions
1 Qt. Tomatoes
1 Pt. Kidney Beans, cooked
12 Ears of Green Corn, kernels removed from ears
8 Oz. Yellow Mustard Seed
4 Oz. Ground Yellow Mustard
1 Lb. Sugar
3 T. Turmeric
2 T. Horseradish, grated
3 T. Celery Seeds
2 T. Olive Oil
1 T. Mace, ground
1 Tsp. Cinnamon
1 T. Cayenne or liquid hot sauce
Vinegar to cover

Peel and slice the cucumbers, sprinkle with salt, and let them stand 6 hours. Prepare the cabbage the same way. Chop the onions, and boil them, covered, for 30 minutes. Chop the tomatoes, beans, corn and scald with boiling water. Drain in a colander. In a large stock pot, mix all the ingredients, except the cucumbers and cabbage. Stir well. Put all the cucumber and cabbage slices in sterilized jars. Put the tomato-corn-spice mixture into the jars in equal amounts. Cover with boiling vinegar and seal. Age 2 weeks.

Salsa de Chile
CHILE SAUCE

50 Tomatoes, ripe, chopped
25 Onions, chopped
12 Green Chiles Serranos, chopped
1 Bunch of Celery, peeled and minced
1½ Gal. Vinegar
3 C. Sugar
1 T. Allspice
1 T. Cloves
1 T. Cinnamon
1 T. Mace
2 T. Salt

Boil all the ingredients 2½ hours. Whirl in blender in batches. Bottle and refrigerate. Sauce is ready for use in 2 weeks.

Chile Mexicano
MEXICAN CHILE SAUCE

No substitutions here. It is rare that good lard can be had. It should not be white. Ideally it should be light brown. Small Mexican *carnicerias* (butcher shops) may have it.

10 Chiles Anchos
10 Chiles Pasillas
1 T. Flour
2 T. Lard
Salt, to taste
2 T. Chorizo
Pinch of Sugar
1 Tsp. Cider Vinegar
1 T. Olive Oil

Toast the chiles until they are pliable. Split and remove stems, seeds and veins. Soak the chiles in a quart of boiling water 10 or 15 minutes. Pass the pulp through a sieve twice, or scrape the meat from the skin. Brown flour in a non-stick sauté pan. Set it aside. Heat the lard to sizzling in another skillet, add the flour to thicken and quickly add the chile pulp. Once boiling, add the salt, chorizo, cider vinegar and olive oil. Cook all together for 15 minutes.

Salsa Nogal
WALNUT SAUCE

2 Tomatoes, peeled
1 Onion, minced
Some Chile Seeds
Walnuts, fresh, chopped

Chop the tomatoes, add the onion and a few chile seeds, season with salt and stew until thick. Strain and add a few chopped fresh walnuts. Reheat and serve hot. Use with fish. This sauce is also used with fried chile dishes, such as Chiles Rellenos.

Salsa Brillante
BRILLIANT SALSA

This sauce is made traditional by the selection of the chiles. Hotter or milder, the choice is the chef's.

2 Lbs. Tomatoes, chopped
1 Oz. Salt
½ Lb. Sugar
16 Oz. Wine Vinegar
½ Lb. Raisins
¼ Lb. Almonds, blanched
1 Oz. Garlic, minced
1 Oz. Ginger, freshly grated
½ Oz. Red Chiles, dried

Boil the tomatoes in very little water. When cooked, run them through a sieve. Put the tomato purée back in the pot. Add to the strained tomatoes the salt, sugar, and vinegar. In a food processor mince the raisins, blanched almonds, garlic, ginger and dried chiles. If the food processor is small, mince as many ingredients at a time as it will hold. Boil all ingredients together until thick.

Salsa Chile de Bernalillo
BERNALILLO CHILE SAUCE

The *Landmark's Club Cook Book*, published in 1902, contained this interesting recipe. Bernalillo is a county in New Mexico.

12 Lg. Tomatoes
12 Green Chiles
12 Med. Onions
3 C. Sugar
3 C. Vinegar
2 Tsp. Allspice
1 Tsp. Chile Cayenne (same as Cayenne powder)
2 Heaping Tsp. Salt

Roast lightly the tomatoes, chiles and onions. Chop well into a stock pot. Add the remaining ingredients, bring to a boil and cook until thick. Bottle in sterilized jars.

Salsa Cocida
COOKED MEXICAN SAUCE

½ C. Olive Oil or Butter
½ C. Onion, minced
½ C. Celery
½ C. Almonds, ground to meal
2 T. Chile Powder
2 T. Paprika
4 C. Tomato purée
2 C. Beef or Chicken Stock
4 Bay Leaves
1 Sprig Mint
Salt and Pepper to taste

Heat the oil in a stock pot, add the onion and celery and sauté lightly. Next add the almond meal, chile powder, paprika and then the tomato purée, beef stock, bay leaves, and mint. Simmer 30 minutes.

PARTY SALSA

A spoonful of this to baste a roast beef adds an excellent flavor. It is also fine with cold boiled ham, fried eggs, or oysters.

24 Red Chiles
Water to cover
½ C. Salt
Mayonnaise
8 Oz. Olive Oil
6 Limes, juiced

To complete the sauce:
Sliced Scallions
Minced Ripe Olives
Salt to taste

Cover the chiles with water, add the salt, and set them on the back of the range where they will keep warm. If your range has a pilotless ignition, put it on the lowest flame possible. Allow to stand until the chiles are soft. Remove from the water with a skimmer. Lay the chiles in a wooden bowl and mash. Rub the stemmed and seeded chiles through a sieve into an earthen bowl, using the back of a metal spoon. Be careful to press through all the pulp. Work this pulp into mayonnaise mixed with the olive oil and the lime juice. This sauce may be bottled and kept cold. When ready to use, add sliced scallions (whites only) and chopped black olives. Salt to taste.

Chile Mostaza
CHILE MUSTARD

3 T. Mustard powder
1 Egg
1 T. Sugar
1 C. Wine vinegar
3 T. Green Chiles, chopped fine
1 T. Olive Oil

Mix the mustard, egg, and sugar. Add to this the vinegar and chiles. Put in a double boiler, stir constantly until thick. When warm, stir in the olive oil.

Salsa de Cahuenga
CHILES CAHUENGA

3 lbs. Green Tomatoes
4 lbs. White Onions
12 oz. Red Hot Chiles (any of the following: jalapeños, serranos, de arbol, piquin, chiltepin)
Salt
Vinegar to cover
2 C. *Piloncillo* or Brown Sugar
2 T. Brown Mustard Seed
1 Tsp. Celery Seed

Soak the whole tomatoes, onion, and chiles overnight in a salt bath. Use 1 C. of salt to 1 gallon of water. Drain, chop the tomatoes, onion and chiles, cover with vinegar, add the sugar, the mustard, and celery seed. Let all come to a boil and bottle while hot.

Salsa de Chile Tostado

TOASTED SALSA ROJA CALIFORNIA

12 New Mexican dried Red Chiles
2 Scallions, minced
3 T. Olive Oil
1 C. Ripe Olives, chopped
1 Tsp. Salt

Toast the chiles and remove the stems, seeds, and veins. In a large kettle, steam the chiles for 30 minutes. Keep the lid on the kettle during this time. Be sure to add enough water to prevent scorching. When the chiles are soft, put them through a food mill or food processor. Don't overprocess. The sauce should not be entirely smooth, more like a purée. Add the cooking water a little at a time, if necessary. Stir in the minced scallions, green and white parts. Add the remaining ingredients. Let chill overnight before serving on roasts or cold meats.

Salsa Para Pescados de la Parilla

GRILL SAUCE FOR FISH

Baste any fish with this sauce.

2 Red Chiles
Salt
1 T. Wine Vinegar
1 Clove Garlic, chopped
1 C. Olive Oil

Soften the chiles in boiling water. Rub them through a sieve, or scrape to obtain the pulp; add a little water, salt and the vinegar. Fry the garlic in a skillet the olive oil, add the chile pulp. Allow to simmer for 30 minutes.

Escabeche Costeño
PACIFIC COAST PICKLE

In late summer, the chiles start to ripen. Use red and green serranos or jalapeños and fresh tomatillos for the pickle below.

1 Quart Cider Vinegar
1 T. Salt
20 Cloves
2 T. Oregano
2 T. Cumin Seed
½ Lb. Fresh Red Chiles
½ Lb. Fresh Green Chiles
1 Lb. Tomatillos
1 Head of Garlic, cloves peeled

Heat a quart of apple vinegar, add a T. of salt, cloves, oregano, cumin seed, boil 5 minutes. Let cool. Pour over small red and green chiles, tomatillos, garlic, and put up in jars. Store in cool, dark place.

Tomate Cimarron Escabeche
WILD TOMATO GRILL SAUCE

Excellent on grilled pork or fish.

4 New Mexican Green Chiles
3 Tomatillos, finely chopped
1 Sm. Onion, minced
1 T. Cilantro (optional)
½ Tsp. Salt

Roast the chiles, then skin, devein and seed them. Allow to cool a little, chop fine. Add the tomatillos, onion, optional cilantro, and salt. Allow the flavors to blend 30 minutes before using.

Entremés Chile y Jitomates Verdes
GREEN CHILE RELISH, NO. 1

Fine over cold meats, fish, oysters, eggs, croquettes, roast pork, mixed with apple sauce or served on fried apple fritters. You may bottle and tightly seal this sauce. It will keep indefinitely.

12 Fresh New Mexican Chiles
1 T. Salt
1 Quart Green Tomatoes
1 C. Cucumber, chopped and seeded
1 Clove of Garlic, minced
½ C. Lime or Lemon Juice
1 T. Salt

Remove seeds and veins from twelve large green chiles, soak overnight in water with one T. of salt in it. Chop and measure one quart green tomatoes. Chop the chiles. Combine tomatoes, chiles, cucumbers, garlic, and cook altogether until a pulp forms. Press through a food mill. Add the lime or lemon juice and salt.

Entremés Chile y Jitomates Rojos
RED CHILE RELISH, NO. 2

12 Fresh Red New Mexican Chiles
1 T. Salt
1 Quart Ripe Tomatoes
1 C. Cucumber, chopped and seeded
1 Clove Garlic, minced
½ C. Lime or Lemon Juice
1 T. Salt

Remove seeds and veins from twelve large fresh red chiles, soak overnight in water with 1 T. of salt in it. Chop and measure one quart ripe tomatoes. Chop the chiles. Combine the tomatoes, cucumber, garlic, and cook altogether until a pulp forms. Press through a food mill. Add lime or lemon juice and salt. You may bottle and tightly seal this sauce. It will keep   indefinitely.

Verduras en Escabeche

SPANISH VEGETABLE PICKLE

This is an excellent way to use up any vegetables left from the garden that you can't use or give away. The trick here is to use a mild vinegar of the best quality. Too sharp a taste will overpower the flavor of the vegetables. Pineapple vinegar would be perfect, but you must make your own.

Vegetables:
2 Heads of Cabbage, finely chopped
18 Cucumbers, sliced and drained
36 Small Pearl Onions, whole
7 New Mexico Green Chiles, chopped

Seasoning:
2 Oz. Yellow Mustard Seed
1 Oz. Celery Seed
1 Oz. Turmeric
2 Lb. Brown Sugar
½ Lb. of Ground Mustard
½ G. Cider or White Wine Vinegar

Chop cabbage fine, cover with salt, mixing well. Allow to stand overnight. In the morning, slice cucumbers about ¼" thick. Salt both sides and allow water to be drawn off. Soak the chiles and the pearl onions in salted water for 4 hours. Drain. Squeeze out excess water with your hands. Mix all the above together. Mix all the herbs and spices together with the cider or wine vinegar. In a kettle put a layer of the mixed vegetables, next sprinkle a layer of the seasoning. Alternate vegetables and vinegar until all are in the kettle. Bring to a slow boil and cook for 30 minutes. When finished cooking, the pickle can be bottled.

Remolachas en Escabeche
MARINATED CALIFORNIA BEETS

1 C. Mayonnaise
1 T. *Tomate Cimarron Escabeche* (see recipe)
Salt and Pepper to taste
1 C. Beets, peeled and diced
1 C. Celery, peeled and diced
½ C. White Onions, minced
½ C. Green Bell Peppers, minced

Blend the mayonnaise, *Tomate Cimarron Escabeche*, salt and pepper. Put the vegetables through a food grinder, or barely chop in a food processor. Mix all together. Serve with meats or on lettuce leaves as a salad.

Rellenos Para Olivos
STUFFING FOR OLIVES

1 Egg Yolk, hard boiled
6 Capers, Californian, chopped fine
1 Heaping T. Parsley, minced
1 Tsp. Butter
1 Tsp. Onion juice
½ Tsp. Anchovy paste

Crumble the yolk with a fork. Add to it the chopped capers, parsley, butter, onion juice and anchovy paste. Stuff the mix into the largest olives available. Measure the onion juice accurately.

Escabeche Mostaza

MUSTARD PICKLES

1 Lb. Yellow Mustard Seed
2 Oz. Turmeric, ground
1½ Gal. Cider Vinegar
4 Oz. Ginger, bruised
2 Oz. Green Chiles, bruised
1 Oz. Garlic
1 Oz. Cloves, whole
1 Oz. Black Pepper, ground
1 Lb. Salt
Cucumbers for pickling
Cauliflower chopped for pickling

Mix the mustard and turmeric with some of the vinegar. When thoroughly mixed, add the remaining vinegar and spices. Bring to a boil, lower heat and gently boil for 15 minutes. Add cucumbers and cauliflower and put in sterilized jars.

Vinaigre Mostaza

MUSTARD VINEGAR

1 T. Mustard Seeds
1 Pt. Cider Vinegar

Pour boiling water into a one pint mason jar, let rest while the vinegar is being simmered. Bruise the mustard seeds and put them in a cheesecloth or cotton infusion bag with a string attached. Pour out the water and place the bag near the bottom of the mason jar, allowing enough room for the vinegar to surround the bag. Keep the string long enough to screw the mason jar lid over it. Bring the vinegar to a simmer. Pour it into the scalded mason jar. Store in a cool, dark place for 10 days, shaking the jar twice or thrice a day. Remove the bag after the tenth day.

Mostaza con Chiles
CHILE MUSTARD

1 C. Mustard powder
5 T. Sugar
5 Eggs
5 C. Wine Vinegar
15 Serrano Chiles, chopped
5 T. Olive Oil

In a double boiler, add the mustard, sugar and eggs. Blend a little. Add the vinegar and chiles. Stir until the mixture thickens. Remove from the heat, cool, and add the olive oil.

Encurdita Mexicana
PICKLED BULL NOSE PEPPERS

Bell peppers were originally called "bull nose peppers."

12 Red Bell Peppers
12 Green Bell Peppers
25 Tsp. Salt
1 Sm. head of Cabbage
1 Tsp. dry Mustard
4 T. Allspice
1 Tsp. Cloves, ground
1 Tsp. Black Pepper
4 C. Vinegar

Carefully remove the top of the peppers. Gently remove the veins and all the seeds. Put 1 Tsp. of salt in each pepper, replace its cap and set all in a stoneware crock for 24 hours. Remove and drain them well. Cut the cabbage as for slaw, mix it with the mustard, spices, and 1 Tsp. of salt. Stuff the slaw into the peppers, recover with the tops, place them back into the crock, and cover with vinegar. Allow to stand 24 hours, and they are ready.

Cure for Ripe Olives

This is a nice recipe because it requires no lye. The olives must be turning reddish black.

1 Five gallon oak barrel or crock
4 Gallons of Ripe Olives
5 C. Rock Salt
Some Bay Leaves

If you have an oaken barrel, put a bung in what will be the bottom when set on its end. This is to allow for easy draining of the water.

Using a stainless steel paring knife, slash the olives on three sides to allow easy marination. Put the olives in the barrel, somewhat neatly, so that all four gallons fit. Cover with fresh water and 4 C. of salt. Change the salt-water every-day for two weeks. This will free the olives from any bitterness. Taste the olives starting after the first week.

Pour a salt brine made of 1 C. of rock salt to 5 gallons of water over the olives, add a few bay leaves (optional). Let this stand three days.

How to Make Oil from Olives

"Cut the olives from the tree when they are quite ripe; keep them for three or four weeks in the dark; mill them; put the paste in sacks, strong but porous; press them and you have oil of the best quality. To have a second grade of oil, put the pressed paste in hot water, and press again. This water, mixed with oil should be put in jars, and when the oil floats to the surface it can be taken off, filtered, and put in bottles. If you add a little salt before the filtering, you will be repaid for the trouble." –From Mrs. Juan Foster in How We Cook in Los Angeles, *1894.*

OLIVE OIL PICKLES

This recipe is from Mrs. Juan Forster. Mr. Forster married into the Bandini family. They owned Rancho Guadalupe, near Los Angeles, that was eleven leagues in size, with 5,000 cattle, 2,000 horses, and sheep too numerous to count. That is just one of the three *ranchos* the Bandini family held. When they were able, the Bandinis held fiestas costing upwards of $2,000 each—probably a million dollars in today's money, as schoolteachers earned about $15.00 per month. That is about eleven years' work, for one party.

1¼ C. Olive Oil
¼ Lb. Black Mustard Seed
¼ Lb. Yellow Mustard Seed
1 T. Celery Salt
2 Tsp. Sugar
100 Cucumber Pickles
Salt
Vinegar

Into a bowl put the olive oil, mustard seeds, celery salt and sugar. Stir and mix together well. Set aside. Cut the cucumbers in thin slices and sprinkle with salt to extract the excess water. Allow to stand overnight. Drain thoroughly and if too salty, rinse and drain well. Put the marinade and cucumber slices into a crock large enough to hold all of them. Mix gently, trying not to break up the slices too much. Pack into sterilized canning jars, top with cold vinegar, and seal.

THE OIL OF CALIFORNIA

In 1800, approximately 500 acres of olive trees were planted by the Spanish Padres. In 1897, 450 of those acres were still producing olives. Olive trees produce progressively more fruit for the first fifty years of their existence, and, after that, the same amount of fruit. With each passing year, however, the fruit becomes more flavorful. The average life of an olive tree is 250 years, but some olive trees growing around Italy date back to the time of Christ.

CHAPTER 3

Appetizers
&
Egg Dishes

Ensalada Escabeche de Lengua
PICKLED TONGUE SALAD

Some people may find the thought of eating tongue distasteful. This is unfortunate because the early pioneers, no matter what their nationality, used all of the food the land and sea provided. There wasn't room for such waste as exists today. Tongue tastes delightful, makes very fine eating, and if you haven't tried it before, this is a good place to start.

1 Tongue medium sized
   (Beef Tongue is readily available at most meatcounters)
1 Tsp. Salt
1 Tsp. Pepper
1 Clove Garlic
1 Bay Laurel Leaf
1 (or more to taste) Chile Pequin or Chiltepin

Dressing:
4 T. Olive Oil
3 T. Wine Vinegar
1 Tsp. Salt
1 Slice of Onion

To a simmering kettle in which the seasonings and spices have been put, add the tongue and slowly boil for 2 to 3 hours. Cool in the cooking liquor. Remove and peel the tongue. The night before you are ready to serve it, slice the tongue thin, pour the dressing over it, and chill overnight. Serve closer to cool than refrigerator cold.

Gorditos
LITTLE FAT ONES

4 C. Masa
Water
½ C. Green Chile Sauce (Sauce No. 2)
½ Lb. Goat Cheese
3 Avocados, sliced
Salt and Pepper to taste

Prepare the masa with water. Don't knead it too much. Allow it to rest, even in the refrigerator, but the dough must be at room temperature before grilling. Hand pat as big as your palm. The finished gordito is about ½ inch thick. Put on a griddle and turning several times, cook until done.

When the tortillas are cool enough, slice into halves. Put the chile sauce, goat cheese, and avocado slices on one side of the tortilla. Spread some more green chile sauce on the other side and put together like a sandwich.

Tacos Queso Fresco
CREAM CHEESE TACOS

To make this recipe as authentic as possible, you must find either real Queso Fresco or a cream cheese with no additives such as gum or other thickeners. Allow the cheese to reach room temperature before mixing.

1 C. Cream Cheese
1 Tsp. Serrano Chile, minced
1 T. Chives, minced or 1 T. Scallions (green part), minced
Salt and Pepper to taste
12 Small Corn Tortillas
1 T. Red Pimiento

In a bowl, mix the cheese, chile, and chives. If you can't find chives, use the green part of the scallions. Add salt and pepper to taste. Warm the tortillas or fry them lightly in olive oil. Spread the cheese mixture over them and dot with red pimento. Serve immediately.

Jaiba con Crema
CREAMED CRAB

2 C. Crab meat, shredded
1 C. Cream
1 Clove Garlic
1 T. Butter
1 T. Flour
1½ C. Milk, hot
Salt and Pepper to taste
Liquid Hot Sauce
Toast rounds

Pour the cream over the crab meat. Set aside. Warm the skillet. Rub the skillet well with the cracked garlic clove. Increase the heat and melt the butter without browning. Add the flour and stir until perfectly smooth. Next, add the hot milk, a little at a time, stirring constantly to thicken. Add the crab and cream and mix well into the cooking sauce. Heat through. Add the salt, pepper, and a dash of the liquid hot sauce, to taste. Serve on toast rounds.

❖

A PILE OF MONEY BUT NO COUTH

A San Francisco funny faux pas story is related by Gertrude Atherton in My San Francisco. *"As the grandfather clock in the hall loudly proclaimed the hour as one, the host stood up and shouted, 'Ladies and gentlemen, I just want to tell you that this is the proudest night of my life. Just thinking that I am entertaining the grand aristocracy [of San Francisco] sends hot chills up and down my spine. I was a long time in making my pile when our home was a shack. Now here I am the proudest man who ever lived. I'm going to bed, but you can stay here all night if you like. And there is plenty more champagne for all. Good night.'" It took more than gold to make gentlemen of the 49ers.*

❖

Berenjena Frito
FRIED EGGPLANT

This dish could double as a vegetable side dish with a meal. It is so simple that it makes a unique appetizer, quite different from the ordinary fried eggplant.

1 Eggplant, peeled, cut in sticks
1 T. Chile Powder
Flour
Olive Oil

Drop the eggplant sticks into boiling water for 10 minutes. Remove and thoroughly drain them. Mix the flour and chile powder and roll the sticks in it. Drop them into a skillet full of hot olive oil and fry to a delicate brown. Drain quickly, lay on a platter and sprinkle with salt. Serve at once.

Tortillas de Papas
POTATO FLAVORED TORTILLAS

1 Lg. Potato, boiled and cold
1 Tsp. Lard, heaping
1 Tsp. Salt
2 C. Flour

Work a large cold boiled potato with 1 Tsp. of lard and 1 Tsp. of salt into the flour and add water until the consistency of bread dough. Knead thoroughly and divide into chunks about the size of an egg. Roll very thin or use a tortilla press. Brown very quickly on a very hot skillet, turning often. When thoroughly cooked, place between a cloth and keep covered in this way until ready to use.

Tortilla Tapatía

OMELET FANDANGO

There is a saying that the best chefs make good omelets. The following recipe will show your culinary acumen and delight your guests or family. Serve as a brunch with champagne and Strawberries in Marsala Wine for dessert.

4 Strips of Bacon
2 Bunches of Scallions
2 Cloves of Garlic, halved
1 T. Green Bell Pepper, minced
1 T. Red Pepper, minced
1 T. Cilantro
16 Black Olives, sliced
16 Seedless Raisins
24 Mushrooms
1 Tsp. Flour
2 C. Tomatoes, chopped, seeded, sieved
Salt to taste
2 T. Chile Powder or 2 T. Chile Sauce No. 1
2 Eggs per person
Cream of Tartar, pinch
Butter for frying

A complete omelet lesson. Fry a strip of bacon for each diner; remove from the fat, place on towel to drain and keep hot in the oven. Add to the hot fat, 4 T. of minced scallions and the slivers of garlic, minced green bell pepper, minced red bell pepper and cilantro, sliced black olives, seedless raisins and mushrooms, sliced. Sauté the mixture until the mushrooms give up their water. When done, add flour to thicken. Then add 2 C. tomato pulp. Cook for a few minutes, salt to taste, add chile powder or red chile sauce No. 1. Use the above amount for every eight eggs. Keep the mixture hot in the oven with the bacon strips.

Prepare the eggs by breaking them and separating the whites and yolks. Beat the yolks first. Add ⅛ C. of water and 1 Tsp. of salt to the yolks. Then beat them until they are very stiff and light in color. Beat the whites stiff, adding a small pinch of cream of tartar while whipping. Fold three-fourths of the whites into the yolks, but do not break them up too fine.

Have a hot omelet pan bottom covered well with butter; pour in the eggs. Lower fire and cook slowly, lifting up with spatula at different places to let raw egg run to the bottom. When nearly done, set under gas broiler or in very hot oven for a few minutes. Next, remove, and with a spoon, put the prepared filling on one-half of omelet, fold other half over, turn out on a hot platter. Put rest of whipped whites on top to form a circular crown around edge. Then sprinkle with more salt and bits of butter; set platter back in oven and brown but not too deeply. Remove and decorate with bits or strips of marinated red bell pepper, sliced black olives, cilantro, and lastly, the strips of bacon and triangles of toast.

Variation: A simple way, not so pretty and fluffy, but good, is to mix the filling with whipped eggs; cook, fold, and serve hot.

AS IS THE CUSTOM OF SMUGGLING

Because of high duties on imports, smuggling became a thriving business in early California. It was known to have taken place at Rancho Palos Verdes, on the bluffs above what is now Marineland. The cove there was used by captains of Yankee clipper ships to smuggle their goods ashore. Don Abel Stearns, husband of Doña Arcadia Bandini, was once accused by the governor of California of being a smuggler. Whether this was true or not, has never been resolved. What is true is that when the time for the re-election of the customs agent came around, the good Don was elected by the people of El Pueblo de Los Angeles. Even the pious padres were forced to resort to purchasing smuggled goods, as they could not obtain paper or ink for the keeping of the Mission records without the Yankee captains' help.

SPANISH STUFFED TOMATO OMELET

1 C. Bread crumbs
½ C. Milk, boiling
1 T. Butter
Salt and Pepper to taste
1 Tsp. Onion Juice
4 Medium Tomatoes, peeled
Eggs
4 Tsp. Chile Pulp or Powder
Butter
Cheese (optional)
Lettuce

Soak the bread crumbs in the boiling milk. Add the butter, salt, black pepper, and fresh onion juice. Peel the tomatoes by dipping in boiling water for 30 seconds. Remove the centers from the peeled tomatoes and stuff with the bread mixture. Place tomatoes on a serving platter, bake until tender. Whip one egg for each tomato separately. Add 1 T. of water to the yolk, salt, 1 Tsp. of chile pepper and 1 Tsp. of butter for each egg. Pour the sauce around the tomatoes to come to the top. Sprinkle with cheese if desired. Bake in moderate oven. Serve hot. Cut tomatoes out in squares to get all the egg and serve on lettuce.

Variation: Partly fill the tomato with bread mixture, break egg on top, sprinkle with cheese and chile powder and bake.

❋

YOU SAY "TOMATE," I SAY "JITOMATE"

The tomato was considered to be poisonous when it was first brought from the New World to the Old. For centuries, it went uneaten. Like Columbus, confounding English with a confusion between Indians (people of the Indian Subcontinent) and Indians (indigenous tribes like the Aztecs or Apaches), the lowly tomato had its nomenclature confounded as well. Spanish differentiates thusly between the fruits: jitomate is the red tomato from the supermarket. Tomate is, in English, the tomatillo or wild tomato. Look for tomatillos in supermarkets. They are a light green to green-yellow and have a papery husk around them.

❋

Huevos Bajos Chile con Queso
EGGS WITH CHILE-CHEESE BLANKETS

    8 Chiles, New Mexican variety
    8 Oz. Monterey Jack Cheese
    Bacon fat
    8 Eggs
    Prepared Spanish Sauce
    Tortillas

Roast, peel and seed the chiles. Cut the Monterey Jack into fingers the length of the chiles, about ¼ inch square. Roll a long piece of cheese in strips of chile, assemble with toothpicks. Fry in hot bacon fat. In another skillet, cook the eggs, *al gusto*. Put eggs on plates, with one cheese and one chile finger. Put in oven to keep hot. Serve with Prepared Spanish Sauce on warmed tortillas.

Tortilla de Huevos con Chorizo
SAUSALITO SAUSAGE OMELET

    4 T. Mexican Chorizo
    4 T. Bread crumbs
    4 T. Milk
    4 Eggs, yolks and whites separated
    Cilantro
    Salt
    4 Tsp. Red Chile Pulp or Powder
    Prepared Spanish Sauce
    Lettuce

Mix the chorizo with the bread crumbs and milk. Whip the yolks of the eggs with a little cilantro, salt, and red chile pepper pulp or chile powder. Whip the whites until frothy but not airy. Add the whites of the eggs to the yolk mixture and pour into a hot greased pan. Cook slowly, until done. Fold and turn out, cover with Prepared Spanish Sauce. Garnish with lettuce and cilantro.

CALIFORNIA CREAMED EGGS

Serves Eight

18 Fresh Eggs
Bechamel Sauce, see below
Butter
Salt
2 T. Paprika
4 T. Cilantro, minced
1 Egg, beaten
Bread crumbs
Olive oil
Toast triangles
Prepared Spanish Sauce

Boil 18 eggs hard (approximately 15 minutes). Shell them and cut lengthwise. Remove the yolks. Mash the yolk and mix with 16 Tsp. of Bechamel Sauce (or bread cooked smooth in milk), bits of butter, salt, paprika, and finely minced cilantro. Fill the whites of the eggs, fasten together with toothpicks. Roll in raw egg and bread crumbs; deep fry in hot olive oil or other fat; drain. Remove toothpicks and if some eggs are cooked together, separate them with a knife and sprinkle with crumbled dry yolk. Pour remaining Bechamel Sauce onto a platter. Make a border of cilantro twigs and egg whites cut in rings. Place toast triangles on platter and put eggs on top. Pour hot Prepared Spanish Sauce partly over and around the eggs. Garnish with more chopped cilantro, and you have a delicious dish in truly Mexican colors.

Bechamel Sauce:
1 C. of Milk
1½ T. Butter
1½ T. Flour
Salt and Pepper to taste
Freshly grated nutmeg

Bring milk to a boil, remove from heat. Simultaneously melt butter in heavy bottomed saucepan over low heat, add flour, stirring briskly. Cook approximately 2 minutes or until it is almost boiling. Remove from heat. Add milk, a little at a time, stirring constantly to keep roux from clumping. Return to heat between additions of milk. When all the milk is added, add salt, pepper and nutmeg. Reduce heat to slow simmer, and stir constantly about 5 minutes. Taste and correct seasonings.

Huevos Mexicanos
MEXICAN SCRAMBLED EGGS IN CHILE

This recipe is so easy. Use the quantity indicated below for each person.

1 Egg per diner
1 T. Green Chile Pulp per diner
1 Tsp. Butter
Garlic slivers or 1 Tsp. Onion Juice per diner
Sauce No. 1
Cilantro

Mix 1 T. of green chile pulp to each egg. Whip each egg separately, then fold in 1 Tsp. of butter, and 1 slice of garlic or 1 Tsp. onion juice. Scramble quickly, serve on toast, garnish with spoonful Red Chile Sauce No. 1 and Cilantro.

Huevos con Chile Rojo en Escabeche
PIMIENTO EGG

Make this for a patio party.

Eggs
Red Chiles, Pickled, or Red Chiles roasted, peeled, seeds
    and stem removed
Salt
Egg for batter
Olive Oil
1 C. Bechamel Sauce (see recipe)
Green Chile Pulp

Hard boil the eggs, shell them, salt them, and place each egg in a piece of red chile. The chile should be large enough to close around the egg and fasten with a toothpick. Dip the wrapped egg in egg batter and deep fry in hot oil or fat. Remove eggs and drain. Slice in half lengthwise. Make 1 C. of Bechamel sauce. Pour sauce on platter, put egg halves on top, flat side up. Add enough green chile pulp to garnish for a beautiful effect.

Huevos en el Horno
SHIRRED EGGS ESPAÑOL

Butter or Bacon Fat
1 Tsp. Onion, minced
1 Tsp. Flour
Salt
1 Tsp. Chile Sauce No. 1
¼ C. Tomatoes, chopped
One Egg and one Ramekin per diner
Cilantro, to garnish

Brown in 1 Tsp. of butter or bacon fat, the minced onion, flour, and salt to taste. Add 1 Tsp. of prepared chile sauce and ¼ C. chopped raw tomato. Cook for a couple of minutes and pour into individual baking dishes (ramekins). Break an egg over top of each ramekin. Set in the oven and bake until the eggs are cooked. Garnish with sprigs of cilantro and serve hot.

Huevos Durango
EGGS DURANGO STYLE

6 Red Chiles
1 T. Olive Oil
½ Med. Onion, chopped
1 Clove, Garlic
1 C. Rice
2 C. Chicken stock
2 T. Butter
Salt to taste
6 Eggs, fresh

Make a pulp of the chiles. Sauté it in olive oil with onion and garlic. Add the rice and cook until dry; then cover with the chicken stock and cook, covered, until tender, about 20 to 25 minutes. Add 2 T. butter and salt to taste. Break the eggs over the rice and scramble in a large non-stick skillet. Serve on a heated platter.
Variation: Omit the eggs and use the rice for stuffing chicken or duck.

Huevos de Señorita Murillo
SENORITA MURILLO'S EGGS

3 Green Chiles
2 T. Olive Oil
6 Slices of Ham, thin
6 Pieces of Toast
6 Eggs
Clarified Butter

Warm the oven. Roast, peel, devein, and remove the stems and seeds from the chiles. Then slice them lengthwise. Heat the olive oil in a sauté pan, add the chiles. Slice the ham very thin, place it in the pan gently. Fry the ham with the chiles for 15 minutes. Make 6 pieces of toast. Put the ham on the toast, the chile strip on the ham and set aside to keep warm. Separately fry the 6 eggs in clarified butter. When cooked *al gusto*, slide eggs onto ham. Serve hot.

Ojos de Buey
EYES OF THE OX

1 T. Flour or 3 T. Toasted Breadcrumbs
12 Red Chiles
2 T. Bacon Fat
1 Tsp. Salt
1 Clove Garlic
1 T. White Wine Vinegar
12 Eggs
2 T. Chives, finely chopped or 2 T. of the whites of Scallions
1 C. Black Olives

Make a red chile pulp from the 12 chiles. Heat the fat in a non-stick skillet, brown the flour or bread crumbs. Mash the garlic clove with the salt; add it to the fat. Pour in the pulp and vinegar. Cook 15 minutes. Pour this purée into a casserole; break the eggs on top of the puree and bake the casserole in a 300 degree oven until the eggs are set. Before serving, garnish with minced chives or scallions and the olives.

Huevos de Caracas
EGGS CARACAS STYLE

3 Green Serrano Chiles, chopped
1 C. Tomatoes
1 Tsp. Butter
1 Tsp. Mustard
Salt
2 Oz. Beef Jerky
3 Eggs
4 Oz. Queso Fresco or Monterey Jack Cheese, grated

Sauté the chopped chiles with the tomatoes, butter, mustard and salt. Cook until the chiles soften. In a dry cast iron skillet, warm the jerky. When it is pliable, shred it as finely as possible, using two forks, or a *metate*. Into a non-stick skillet, add the eggs, shredded jerky, and chile-mustard mix. Scramble until the eggs are cooked and sprinkle the cheese over the mixture. Serve with toasted bread.

Huevos Poblanos
EGGS MOLE

1 Jar Mole Sauce
1½ C. Meat Stock
½ C. Olive Oil
6 Eggs
1 T. Cilantro, minced
Salt and Pepper to taste

Mix the mole sauce in the warm stock. Add the olive oil and and bring the pot to a simmer for 10 minutes. Remove from heat. Pour the sauce in an enameled casserole. Poach the eggs in the mixture, covered, taking care not to break the yolks. Sprinkly with cilantro and salt and pepper. Serve hot with Mexican style sweet pastries and Ybarra Hot Chocolate.

Fritada California
MEXICAN FRENCH TOAST

1 Egg
2 T. Cream
Dash Nutmeg
Dash Cinnamon
1 Tsp. Sugar
1 French Baguette or Mexican Bolillos
Olive Oil and Butter
Wine Syrup or Simple Syrup

Beat the egg with the cream, nutmeg, cinnamon, and sugar. Cut the bread into lengths as thick as a finger. Soak the bread in the egg mixture and fry to a nice brown in oil and butter. Serve at once with wine syrup or simple syrup.

Wine syrup:
Use any wine in place of water with sugar to make a simple syrup. Flavor with lemon or orange slices during the simmer. Remove the citrus slices before bottling.

EGGS AS GOOD AS GOLD

During the Gold Rush, eggs brought as much as $6.00 per dozen. Sometimes the price reached $12.00 per dozen. During one of those times, a mercantile agent embarked for San Francisco. Upon arriving there, he sold his eggs for $4.00 per dozen. He felt he had made a handsome profit. However, quickly learning that eggs were going for more, he bought them back and resold them the same day for a greater profit.

Mount Shasta, Siskiyou County, rising 14,000 feet above sea level
Paul Elder Publishing, Circa 1911

CHAPTER 4

Salads
&
Dressings

Californio Aderezo
CALIFORNIA SALAD VINEGAR

1 Clove Garlic
1 Slice Cucumber
1 Onion slice, Red or White, not yellow
1 T. Cilantro or Parsley
1 T. fresh Tarragon leaves
1 Pint Rice Vinegar

Put a clove of garlic, a large slice of cucumber, a slice of onion, 1 T. cilantro or parsley, 1 T. tarragon leaves, or 2 T. tarragon vinegar into one pint rice vinegar. Bottle and let stand several days, strain, and use for the following salads, dressings, and other recipes.

EARLY L.A. ELECTORAL PROCESS

In the early days of El Pueblo Nuestra Señora de Los Angeles de Porciuncula de Los Temblores (as Los Angeles was known then), voting was not as orderly as it could have been. Mexican immigrants, as well as tribes of Indians, voted only when the candidates saw fit. The usual manner of business was for the candidate and his henchmen to round up various strangers, stragglers, and Indians and herd them into corrals. Once there, these potential votes were kept in a truly magnificent state of intoxication until the polls opened. Then they were put in stages hired from Phineas Banning. Transported to the polls, they were turned over to friends of the candidate and led to the voting booth to cast their inebriated ballot, like so many inanimate objects. Having served their usefulness, they were then free to go, until the next election, unless they were rounded up and corralled to vote a second or third time that day. —From Reminiscences of a Ranger, by Horace Bell.

CALIFORNIA GREEN CHILE MAYO WITH VINEGAR

1 Clove Garlic
1 Egg
¼ C. Best Olive Oil
¼ C. Lemon Juice
1 T. White Wine Vinegar
1 Tsp. Sugar
½ Tsp. Salt
1 T. Green Chile Pulp

Rub a mixing bowl with a clove of garlic. Break into the bowl one egg yolk and whip it until stiff. Very slowly add the olive oil, lemon juice, vinegar, sugar, salt, and green chile pulp. Stir gently and serve.

No. 2

CALIFORNIA CREAMY CHILE DRESSING

6 T. Best Olive Oil
3 T. Fresh Lemon Juice
1 T. California Salad Vinegar (see recipe this chapter)
1 Tsp. Brown Sugar
½ Tsp. Salt
1 T. Red Chile Pulp

Put six tablespoons of best olive oil in a mixing bowl. Add gradually, lemon juice, California Salad Vinegar, brown sugar, salt, and a tablespoon of red chile pulp. Whisk with a rotary motion until thick and creamy. Serve at once on any salad.

No. 3

CALIFORNIA SPICY DRESSING

6 T. Fresh Lime Juice
3 T. Best Olive Oil
1 Tsp. Sugar
½ Tsp. Salt
Dash of Chile Piquin, Arbol, Chipotle, Chiltepin, or whatever
 powder is on hand
1 Tsp. Onion Juice

Put the lime juice in a mixing bowl. Add the olive oil, sugar, salt, a dash red pepper, 1 Tsp. onion juice. Mix well.

AVOCADO SALAD

Bertha Ginger described this salad as "exciting."

2 Ripe Haas Avocados
Salt
Sugar
Lettuce
½ C. No. 3 Dressing

Peel the avocados and cut them in half. Sprinkle with salt and sugar 20 minutes before using, then place them in the heart of crispy lettuce head, pour Dressing No. 3 over and serve.

Aguacates Rellenos

STUFFED AVOCADOS

4 Oz. Pork, ground
2 T. Olive Oil
1 C. Tomatoes, minced
1 T. Black Olives, minced
1 Tsp. Capers
¼ T. Green Chile pulp
1 Clove Garlic
4 Whole Cloves
1 T. Almonds, minced
1 T. Salted, shelled Pine Nuts (Piñones)
Dash Cinnamon
1 T. Cilantro, minced
3 Avocados
1 Egg

Salt and pepper the pork and fry lightly in the oil; add tomatoes, olives, capers, chile, garlic, cloves and simmer until tender, about 20 minutes. Then add the nuts, cinnamon, and cilantro, stir and set aside. Peel the avocados, slice into halves, place in a casserole and fill with the simmered mixture. Lightly beat the egg with 1 T. of water and pour over the avocados. Heat in a 300 degree oven until the egg is set. Remove and allow to cool a little.

ORANGES AND LEMONS

In 1873, L.C. Tibbetts of Riverside received two Navel orange trees from Bahia, Brazil. This Washington Navel, became the favorite of the nation. In 1895, Southern California had 397,792 lemon trees, producing 800 railroad carloads a year for shipment back east. The Lisbon and the Eureka were the leading varieties of lemons.

Ensalada de Congrego
COMBINATION SALAD

In *El Cocinero Espagñol*, Encarnacion Pinedo has two salads that typify the brilliance of Californio cuisine. Crab meat deserves the shallots, but perhaps the market is out of them. In that case, use garlic.

1 C. cooked Crab Meat, chilled and chopped
Olive Oil, to taste
1 Tsp. White Wine Vinegar, Tarragon Vinegar or California Salad Vinegar
Black Pepper
Salt
Shallots, chopped, or Garlic
Lettuce, chopped

To the chopped crab meat, add the olive oil, vinegar, pepper, salt and shallots, with an equal amount of lettuce. Serve immediately.

TOMATO AND CUCUMBER SALAD

6 Ripe Tomatoes
2 Cucumbers
½ C. Dressing No. 3
Lettuce leaves
½ C. Green Bell Pepper, thinly sliced

Peel, core, and coarsely chop 2 tomatoes. Place in a bowl in the refrigerator. Pare the cucumbers and chop them finely. Mix the cucumbers with the tomatoes. Pour Dressing No. 3 over the mixture. Core the remaining tomatoes, cut a slice off the top of them, and with a spoon remove the tomato pulp from each tomato. Fill the tomatoes with the tomato-cucumber mixture. Arrange lettuce leaves on a plate, set the stuffed tomatoes on top, and garnish with the bell pepper slices.

Variation: Use thinly sliced New Mexican chiles for a spicier garnish.

Ensalada Chile Dulce
California Sweet Pepper Salad

2 Green or Red Bell Peppers, cut into halves
1 Large Cucumber, pared and chopped
4 Celery Stalks, peeled and chopped
½ C. Dressing No. 3
Pimiento or Pickled Beets for garnish
Lettuce leaves

Remove the seeds from the peppers and fill with peeled, chopped cucumber and celery, mixed with dressing No. 3. Garnish with pimiento or sliced, pickled beets. Serve on lettuce.

Bean Salad

1 C. Pink Beans, cooked (or Kidney Beans)
½ C. New Mexican Chile, chopped
¼ C. Onion, chopped
¼ C. Red bell pepper, chopped
¼ C. Cilantro, chopped
¼ C. Cucumber, chopped
¼ - ½ C. Dressing No. 1
Parsley

Combine all the ingredients and serve garnished with chopped parsley.

Spanish Tomato and Egg Salad

4 Large Tomatoes, sliced
Lettuce Leaves
4 Eggs, hardboiled
½ C. Dressing No. 1

Blanch the tomatoes. Peel, core, and slice them in three slices across. Place on lettuce leaves. Put a border of hard boiled egg whites around the edge of the plate. Place the yolks in the center of the slices, pour Dressing No. 1. over the plate and serve slightly chilled.

Stuffed Tomato Salad

2 Large Ripe Tomatoes
½ C. Celery, chopped
½ C. New Mexican Chile, chopped
½ C. Onions, chopped
Olive Oil
Lemon Juice
Salt
½ C. Dressing No. 1
½ C. Monterey Jack or Longhorn cheese, grated
Cilantro

Blanch, peel and core the tomatoes. Gently remove the center and chop. Mix that with equal parts of celery, green chile, and onions. Fry all in little olive oil and lemon juice, add salt to taste. Refill the tomato shells with the mixture and a teaspoon of Dressing No. 1. Sprinkle a little grated cheese and chopped cilantro on top. Serve on lettuce.

CALIFORNIO RIPE OLIVE SALAD

1 Pint Cottage Cheese
1 T. Pimiento
1 Tsp. Salt
2 Tsp. Paprika
2 T. Cilantro, minced
1 Jar Largest Black Pitted Olives available
Lettuce
½ C. Dressing No. 1

Make a mixture of cottage cheese, pimento, salt, paprika, cilantro to taste. Stuff the olives. Serve on lettuce, covered with Dressing No. 1.

SPANISH MOLDED SALAD

1 C. Tomatoes, chopped
½ C. Cucumber, chopped
½ C. Celery, chopped
¼ C. Green Bell Pepper, chopped
1 T. Onion, chopped
½ Tsp. Chile Powder
Salt
1 T. Unflavored gelatin
1 C. Tomato Juice
½ C. Dressing No. 1 or 2

Chop enough ripe tomatoes to fill a cup, mix with cucumber, celery, green bell peppers, onion, chile powder and salt to taste. Dissolve one tablespoon gelatin in one cup tomato juice, pour over above, mix and put in a mold. When, firm cut in squares, serve with California Sauce Nos. 1 or 2 on lettuce leaves.

Spanish Cucumber and Tomato Salad

1 Large Cucumber
1 Pint Cabbage
1 large Tomato
1 Green Bell Pepper
¼ C. Onion Juice
½ C. Dressing No. 2 `

Pare and chop fine one good sized fresh cucumber, let drain. Shred sufficient cabbage to make one pint. Place the cabbage in cold water for 1 hour. Blanch and peel one good sized tomato and chop it fine. Remove the seeds from one large sweet pepper, chop it fine, and mix with the tomato. When ready to serve, drain and dry the cabbage. Put into a glass salad bowl, a layer of cucumber cubes, then a layer of chopped tomato and pepper; sprinkle with a few drops of onion juice. Then a layer of cabbage and continue until all the material is used. Serve with Dressing No. 2.

Ensalada Encolerizarse
Spanish Cabbage Salad

1 C. Red Cabbage
1 C. White Cabbage
2 T. Chestnuts, roasted and chopped
2 T. Pecans, chopped
½ C. Dressing No. 2
Lettuce

Mix the red and white shredded cabbage together. Add the chestnuts, and pecans. Mix with Spanish Dressing No. 2 and serve in lettuce cups.

RICE SALAD

Lettuce leaves
1 C. Cooked Rice
1 Small head Iceberg Lettuce, shredded
¼ C. Cabbage, shredded
4 Eggs, hardboiled and sliced
Dressing No. 1
1 Hard boiled egg yolk
Chives, minced
Radishes, slices
¼ C. Heavy Cream
Dressing No. 3

Arrange the some lettuce leaves on a platter and spread the rice over them. Add the shredded lettuce and cabbage and then the slices of hard-boiled eggs and top with a little Spanish Dressing No. 1. Over the top layer of dressing press the hard boiled egg yolk through a coarse sieve and sprinkle. Garnish with the chives and radishes. Next, add ¼ C. cream to ½ C. Dressing No. 3 pour over the salad and serve.

Ensalada de Verdolagas
PURSLANE LEAF SALAD

Purslane is a weed most folks would like to get rid of. Since it is edible, this is an excellent way to accomplish that task. Purslane is also called Pigweed. This recipe is from *Early California Hospitality*, by Ana Bégué de Packman.

2 Lbs. Purslane leaves
3 T. Olive Oil
2 T. Wine Vinegar
½ Tsp. Salt
¼ Tsp. Black Pepper
1 Medium sized sliced Onion

Clean and wash the purslane. Cook until tender in a quart of simmering water. Drain thoroughly. Beat the olive oil, wine vinegar, and salt and pepper together. Toss the purslane and sliced onions, then coat with the dressing. Chill before serving.

Ensalada con Camarones

CALIFORNIO SHRIMP SALAD

4 Eggs, hard boiled, whites and yolks separated
Olive Oil
½ Tsp. Dijon-style Mustard
4-6 T. White Wine Vinegar
Salt and Pepper to taste
Lettuce
1 C. Shrimp, cooked *al gusto*
1 Clove Garlic, chopped
Chervil

Mash the egg yolks and mix with olive oil and the mustard to form a thick paste. Add the vinegar, salt and pepper. Chop the whites coarsely, chop the lettuce to bite size. Fold the shrimp into the egg yolk. Then mix the shrimp mixture into the lettuce and egg whites. Add the chopped garlic and fresh chervil to taste. Toss the salad well and serve on lettuce leaves.

Ensalada Plátano

WALNUT SALAD WITH CHILE BANANAS

Hot Chile powder, cayenne, or piquin, to taste
1 C. Mayonnaise
1½ C. Walnuts
4 Bananas, just ripe (not soft)
Lettuce leaves

Mix the hot chile powder with the mayonnaise, put back in the refrigerator to meld the flavors. Finely chop the nut meat in a food processor. Cut the bananas in thin slices. Fold the nuts into the slices. On a serving platter covered with lettuce leaves, mound the banana-nut mix. Pour the chile-mayonnaise sauce over all.

Pollo Monterey
CHICKEN SALAD

2 Eggs, hard boiled
2 C. Chicken, cooked
6 Green Chiles, roasted, peeled, and chopped
1 C. Celery, peeled, and chopped
1 C. Ripe Olives
Oregano, to taste (optional)

Combine all ingredients in a bowl and mix.

Salad Dressing:
2 T. Butter
1 T. Sugar
1 Tsp. Salt
2 Tsp. Dijon-style Mustard
1 C. Wine Vinegar
1 Egg, beaten

In a saucepan, combine all the ingredients. Bring to a boil over a low heat. Remove and chill. When cold, pour over the chicken salad.

THE HIGH-AND LOW-COST OF COMMUNICATION

Telegraph rates in 1869 were exorbitant. Ten words sent from San Francisco to Los Angeles cost one dollar and a half. By comparison, letters back to the East cost between two and four cents each, and it was thought that the ships carrying the letters going around the Horn were doing a booming post office business of twelve to fifteen dollars per trip.

The chuckwagon cook wearing sombrero

CHAPTER 5

Soups

&

Chile con Carne

Sopa de Frijoles
BEAN SOUP

Traditionally, stews and soups were done in a clay pot *olla* or *puchero*. *Ollas* are available wherever there are large Mexican communities. Do not purchase a glazed pot.

1 Pint Pinto Beans
2 Qts. Beef Stock
1 C. Onions, chopped
4 Chiles, Green or Red, Fresh (roasted and peeled) or Canned
1 Qt. Tomatoes, canned
2 T. Cilantro, chopped
Albondigas (see recipes below)
Cheese Fingers

Cook pink pinto beans in the beef stock until tender. Add the chopped onions, 2 green and 2 red chiles, tomatoes, and cilantro. Cook all thoroughly. Drop in Spanish meat balls, *albondigas*, and serve with Spanish Cheese Fingers.

Albondigas
SPANISH MEAT BALLS FOR SOUP

1 Lb. Stew Beef
2 Eggs
1 Tsp. Salt
2 T. Onion Juice
4 T. Bread, chopped fine and soaked in beer, wine, or milk
3 T. Cilantro finely chopped
3 T. Pimiento, minced
Olive oil for frying
Toasted Bread Crumbs

Grind stew beef very fine in a food processor, but do not puree. Add to it the eggs, salt, onion juice, and 4 T. of bread soaked in beer, wine or milk. Make the mixture into 1 inch diameter balls. Roll in the chopped cilantro and the minced pimiento for a colorful effect and lastly in the bread crumbs. Fry in oil and drain. Drop in bean soup just before serving.

Variation: Use 1 lb. of chicken meat and use mint instead of cilantro. Or use half each of both cilantro and mint, for either the beef or the chicken.

Sopa de Papas
POTATO SOUP

1 C. Mashed Potatoes
1 C. Soup Stock
1 C. Milk
1 T. Butter
Salt to taste
1 Bay Laurel Leaf
1 T. Flour
Bread, thinly sliced for rounds
Butter
Cheddar Cheese
Red Bell Pepper, minced
Cilantro, minced

Add 1 C. mashed potatoes to 1 C. chicken, veal or beef stock. Add the milk, butter, salt to taste, bay laurel leaf, and 1 T. flour to thicken and cook. Run the soup through a food mill and reheat. Cut thinly sliced bread rounds, the size of a quarter, butter and toast then. Make a little pile of grated yellow cheese on the toast rounds. Top them with some roasted and marinated red bell pepper. Garnish with a pinch of chopped cilantro on top. Serve the soup hot with the toast on top.

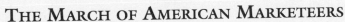

THE MARCH OF AMERICAN MARKETEERS

Hugo Perfecto Reid, a Scotsman, came to Los Angeles in 1824 and opened the first general store on the American plan. In 1831, with the opening of the Santa Fé Trail, (sometimes called the Old Spanish trail), the means of developing an extensive trade began. Mules were sent from California in exchange for the fine serapes or blankets of the Rio Grande Valley. In 1853, there were three dry goods stores in LA. In 1854, the population numbered 4,000, of whom 500 were Americans. All the stores were run by Anglos.

Caldo Caliente
HOT VEGETABLE BROTH

1 C. Cabbage, shredded
1 C. Carrots, chopped
½ C. Onions, chopped
1 C. Garlic, chopped
½ C. Turnips, chopped
½ C. Celery, peeled and chopped
¼ C. Green New Mexican Chiles, chopped
1 Qt. Canned Tomatoes
1 Qt. Meat Stock
Cooked Rice

Make a broth of shredded cabbage, carrots, onions, garlic, turnips, chopped celery, chiles, canned tomatoes, and clarified meat stock. Cook thoroughly until vegetables are cooked, strain, and serve hot with a spoonful of cooked rice in a soup bowl.

Variation: For vegetable soup, leave all the vegetables in.

Sancocho de Pescado
MONTEREY FISH CHOWDER

½ C. Salt Pork, cubed
½ C. Onion, chopped
1 T. Flour
2 C. White Fish meat, boned
2 C. Milk, hot
1 C. Prepared Spanish Sauce
Salt
Paprika

Fry the salt pork and the chopped onion together and brown lightly. Add the flour, stir, then add the fish meat and brown slightly. Add the hot milk and the Prepared Spanish Sauce, with salt to taste. Cook until slightly thickened. Garnish with a dash of paprika.

Variation: Clams or oysters may be used, allowing just 1 minute for cooking them.

Frijoles Negroes
BLACK BEANS IN WINE WITH LEMON

2 C. Black Beans
4 C. Water
8 C. Beef Stock
2 Eggs, hardboiled and sliced
1 Lemon, sliced
1 C. dry Sherry (not cooking sherry)
Salt and pepper to taste

Put the beans in a pot and cover with 4 C. water. Bring to a boil and then lower to a simmer. Cook for 3 to 4 hours. Run the beans, drained, through a food mill. Return the beans to the pot. Add the stock and return the beans to a boil. Add the salt and pepper and cook until slightly thickened. In the bottom of a soup tureen, place the sliced eggs and lemon slices. Add the sherry and bean purée and allow to stand 5 minutes. Serve with tortillas.

Sopa Jalisciense
JALISCO STYLE SOUP

1 Lb. Ground Round Steak
3 Slices of Bread, wetted in milk, beer or wine
2 Eggs
1 Small Onion, finely chopped
Salt
Pepper
3 T. Olive Oil
½ C. Flour
1 C. canned Chile Sauce (Ortega Brand)
Several Mint Leaves, well chopped
5 C. Water
Salt

Mix the meat, wetted bread, eggs, onion, salt, and pepper together and make meatballs. Set them aside. Brown the flour in the oil. Add the canned sauce and mint, the water and the salt. Boil all together for 20 minutes. Drop the meatballs into the boiling broth, one by one, and allow to boil 15 minutes. The meatballs could be made ahead.

Sopa Almendra
ALMOND SOUP

    1 C. Rice
    1½ Qts. Milk
    8 Oz. Almonds without skins
    ½ C. Cream
    1 T. Sugar
    Chile Powder to taste
    Salt

Put the rice and 1 quart of milk in a double boiler. Cook slowly until every grain is tender. In a food processor, with the steel knife, add the almonds, and grind to a powder, then slowly, drop by drop, add the cream. This will make a smooth paste. Add the sugar, chile powder, and a pint of milk. Blend again, very briefly. Put the almond-chile paste into the rice and simmer for 30 minutes. Season with salt and if too thick, add more milk.

Caldo de Pescado
FISH BROTH SOUP

Almost any fish can be used here. Perhaps red snapper for economy or salmon for extravagance. For the Bouquet Garni: In a cheesecloth bag, put 1 bay leaf, 1 sprig fresh or ¼ tsp. dry thyme and ½ tsp. of minced parsley.

    4 Sm. Onions, chopped
    4 T. Olive Oil
    6 Tomatoes, peeled and chopped
    1 Bouquet Garni
    1 Parsley Sprig
    1 Wineglass of White Wine
    4 T. Olive Oil
    1 Green Chile
    4 T. Flour
    6 fillets Fish (almost any variety), sliced thin

Chop the onions and sauté in 4 T. of oil. Add the tomatoes and the bouquet garni, the parsley, the wine, 4 moreT. of oil, the chile, and the flour. Cook for 10 minutes and add 3 pints of water and boil for 30 minutes. Then add the fish slices and simmer 5 to 10 minutes, depending on the fish. Remove the bouquet garni, taste for salt, serve in bowls over dry crusts of bread.

Sopa Espasa de Chilitos
CHILE BISQUE

1 C. Red Chile Pulp
1 C. Rice, cooked
Liquid Hot Sauce
Salt
1 Egg
½ C. Cream
1 Qt. Milk, heated
Toast Squares

Combine the pulp and the rice in a blender or food processor and make a smooth sauce. Season this sauce highly with the hot sauce and add salt to taste. Beat the egg with the cream and add to 1 quart of hot milk. Blend the chile-rice mixture into the milk, heat, and serve over squares of toast.

Sopa Primavera de Cordero
SPRING LAMB SOUP

1 Lb. Spring Lamb, cubed
1 Med. Onion, sliced
Lard or Oil
3 Tomatoes, peeled and sliced
3 Green New Mexican Chiles, roasted, peeled, and finely chopped
2 Qts. Water
1 C. Green Peas
1 C. Corn (cut from the cob—no substitutions)
½ C. Rice
Salt
1 Serrano Chile, minced
1 Egg, beaten
1 Tsp. Olive Oil
½ Tsp. Vinegar

Sauté the lamb with the onion in lard or oil. When nicely browned, add 3 peeled and sliced tomatoes and 3 green chiles, finely chopped. Cover with 2 quarts of water and simmer slowly approximately 20 to 30 minutes. Add the green peas, corn, rice, salt, and minced chile serrano, and simmer for 15 minutes. In a small bowl or glass, work into the egg ½ Tsp. vinegar and 1 Tsp. olive oil. Put the egg mixture in the bottom of a soup tureen and pour the soup over it and serve.

Gitano Puchero
GYPSY STEW

3 Qts. Beef Stock
1 Onion
4 Cloves Garlic, peeled
2 Oz. Salt Pork
8 Oz. Mexican Red Beans (not pinto beans), soaked overnight, then cooked until tender
1 Lb. Salted Codfish (soaked overnight)
4 Oz. Chorizo
2-4 New Potatoes, diced

Into the stock, put the onion, garlic, and salt pork. To this add the beans and salt codfish. Simmer slowly and when partly done in about 8 minutes, add the chorizo and the diced potatoes. Cook another 8 to 12 minutes.

Tallarínes Puerta de Oro
NOODLES SAN FRANCISCO

This recipe would have been made with *cotija* cheese. This is a dry, crumbly cheese with a tangy taste somewhat like Parmesan. If *cotija* is not readily available, Parmesan will just have to do.

1 C. Cotija cheese, grated
1 C. Flour
Salt
Powdered Cayenne or Piquin to taste
4 Eggs
½ C. Cream
Pot of boiling stock

Into a large bowl, put the finely grated cheese, flour, salt and chile powder. In a bowl or glass, mix up the eggs and cream and beat. Add the egg-cream mixture to the flour-cheese mixture. This should make a thin batter. Over the boiling stock, hold a colander or very coarse strainer, pour the batter into the stock this way. This will form long strings which must boil 10 minutes.

Sopa Rancheros de Campos
COUNTRY RANCH SOUP

1 C. Onion, minced
1 C. Vegetables, minced (Carrots, Potatoes, Turnips)
1 C. Butter, scant
1 C. Flour
2 C. Canned, Stewed Tomatoes (use one 15 oz. can)
8 Cloves
3 Qts. Soup Stock (Beef or Vegetable)
½ Bay Laurel Leaf
1 Tsp. Chile Piquin or Cayenne powder
Salt

Sauté the onion and vegetables in the butter, and when light brown, mix in the flour and transfer to a 350 degree oven for 20 minutes to brown through without scorching. While the vegetables are finishing, take the stewed tomatoes and cloves and heat in a skillet to dry them out. Dry them to the point where the liquid is almost, but not completely gone, just enough to concentrate the flavors. Set this skillet aside, if you finish before the vegetables are ready. Scrape the contents of the baked vegetables into 3 quarts of soup stock and add the stewed tomatoes, the cloves, just ½ of a bay laurel leaf and chile powder. Simmer for 1 hour, skimming occasionally and season well with salt.

Sopa de Carne Seca y Arroz
BEEF JERKY SOUP

3 Oz. Beef Jerky
1 T. Cooking Oil
½ C. Rice
1 Lg. Tomato, ripe
1 Green Chile, roasted, peeled, and chopped
1 Med. Onion
¼ Tsp. Pepper
Salt
1 Qt. Water, boiling

In a non-stick skillet, roast the meat to soften it. In a mortar, preferably a *metate*, grind the meat to fine shreds. Heat the oil in a stew pot and sauté the rice, tomato, chile, and onion. Add salt and pepper. Add the shredded meat and 1 quart of boiling water and simmer until rice is done, 15 to 20 minutes.

Olla Podrida de la Madrid

OLD STYLE SAVORY STEW

1½ Lbs. each cubed Mutton, Veal, Pork
1 thin slice of Ham
1½ Lbs. Garbanzo Beans
Salt to taste
3 Dry Red Chiles
1 Clove Garlic, toasted and peeled
½ C. each of the following Summer Vegetables: Green Peas, Lima Beans, Squash, Onions, String Beans, Corn
2-4 Oz. *longaniza* sausage, sliced ½ inch thick

For the Sauce:
1 C. of the stock
3 Tomatoes, stewed and strained
A pinch of Cumin Seeds, toasted
Pepper
2 T. Wine Vinegar

In a large stock pot put the cubed mutton, veal, pork. Next add the whole ham slice and garbanzos. Cover with 1 gallon of water. Add the salt, red chiles, and garlic, and bring to a boil. Skim and cook slowly until the meat is almost tender, then draw off 1 cup for the sauce.

Drop the vegetables into a separate stock pot with water to simmer for 25 minutes. Five minutes before serving add the *longaniza*.

Place the meat on a large platter and surround it with the cooked vegetables. Serve the sauce in a sauceboat and pour over the meat and vegetables.
To make the Sauce:

Stew and strain 3 tomatoes, add 1 C. of broth, a pinch of cumin seeds, salt, pepper, and the vinegar. Bring to a boil and serve.

Puchero
A BOILED POT

1 Knuckle Bone, sun and air dried
2 Lbs. each cubed Veal and Beef
3 Ears of Corn
1 C. Garbanzo Beans
2 Onions, whole
3 Tomatoes, dried
2 Green Chiles
1 Lb. Snap Beans, tied in bunches
1 Bundle Kohlrabi leaves
3 Summer Squash
1 Apple, unripe
1 Pear, unripe
2 Tsp. Salt
½ Tsp. Pepper

In a large stock pot, cover the meat and knuckle bone with cold water. Bring to a boil and skim. Place all the vegetables and fruit over the meat and bone. The vegetables and fruits must be placed into the pot in the order that they are given in the ingredients listing. That is necessary so that they will cook whole. Simmer for 3 hours. Never stir.

To serve, lift out the whole vegetables and fruits onto a platter. Chop the vegetables and fruits. Onto a separate platter, place the meat. Now strain the broth into a soup tureen. In bowls, combine the meats, fruits, and vegetables, and pour the broth over it.

Sopa de Jitomate
CALIFORNIO TOMATO SOUP

2½ C. Fresh Tomatoes, peeled and chopped
2 Onions, chopped fine
2 Bay Laurel Leaves
1 Clove Garlic
3 C. Water
¼ Lb. Carrots, sliced
6 Red Chiles
2 Sprigs, Thyme
1 Sprig, Marjoram
2 Chickens, cut for as for frying

Cook all ingredients except the chicken together for 30 minutes. Strain the liquid into a stockpot. Add the cut up chicken pieces. Cook uncovered until chicken is well done. Remove meat to cool, chop and use for chicken salad. Put the broth in a double boiler to keep warm. Add some freshly fried croutons, just before serving.

Menudo
TRIPE SOUP

3 T. Butter
½ C. Chopped Onion
1 Lb. Honeycomb Beef Tripe cut into strips 1 x ½ inches, salted
Flour
1 C. Chopped Tomatoes
Chile Pulp or Powder (to taste)
1 Tsp. Sugar

Garnish:
Lemon Wedges, Oregano Leaf, Chile Piquin and Chopped Onion.

In the butter, fry the onion until lightly browned. Roll the tripe in the flour. Brown the tripe in the hot oil. Add to this 1 C. chopped tomatoes, enough water to cover, season with 1 T. chile pulp or powder and 1 Tsp. sugar. Let simmer slowly until very tender, 2 to 3 hours. Serve hot with the garnishes.

Menudo Feliz Navidad

CHRISTMAS DAWN MENUDO

A fancier menudo. A traditional Christmas Dawn repast, after Midnight Mass, would be made as follows.

3 Lbs. Tripe
1 Hoof and shank of veal
2 Lbs. of hominy
1 Med. Onion, chopped
1 Clove Garlic, peeled
1 T. Red Chile powder
3 Stalks of Mint
12 Leaves of Cilantro
2 Tsp. Salt
½ Tsp. Pepper

Wash the tripe and veal hoof and shank in several changes of water until the water clears. Into a stockpot, put the meats and hominy. Add enough water to cover and 1 inch more. Boil and skim thoroughly. Cook at a low boil for 3 hours or until ingredients are well done. Set aside overnight. Skim the fat; reserve 2 T. of it. To prepare for serving, cut the tripe and jellied veal into bite size cubes.

Heat in the stockpot 2 T. of the fat which formed on the meat overnight. Add the onion, garlic, chile, mint, and cilantro. Fry slowly. Then add the meat, jellied broth, and hominy. Simmer for 30 minutes. Serve in deep bowls. Season with salt and pepper to taste.

Sopa de Crema Sylvia

SYLVIA'S SOUP

½ C. White Beans
10 Chicken feet
2 Lbs. Leg of Beef with bone
¼ Lb. Marrow Soup bone
¼ Lb. Beef Ribs
1 Lg. Leek
1 Young Cabbage
2 Lg. Turnips
3 Carrots
3 Onions
Salt
Pepper
6 Celery Leaves
6 Green Chiles
4 Qts. Water
4 Oz. Chorizo
1 Slice Pork
1 Bay Laurel Leaf
2 Pig's Feet, for garnish

Soak the white beans overnight. Discard the soaking liquid. Remove the nails and skin from the chicken feet. Use a vegetable brush to clean the vegetable skins. Place the chicken feet, beef, soup bone, ribs, vegetables, salt, and pepper in a stockpot and cover with cold water. Cover and bring to a simmer for 6 hours. *Do not skim*. In a small clay pot, simmer 1 quart of water, beans, chorizo, pork, and bay leaf for 5 hours, or until all most all the water has evaporated. When the water has evaporated, grind the beans and sausage in a mortar, or put through a meat grinder. Return the ground mixture to a saucepan and add 1½ quarts of the prepared soup stock. Pass this all through a colander. Put in a double boiler to keep hot before serving. To garnish, cook the pig's feet and when done, divide into small pieces and place around the dish.

Sopa de Ajos con Huevos
BAKED EGGS IN GARLIC SOUP

2 Lbs. Soup marrow bones
1 Lg. Onion, finely chopped
4 Med. Carrots, peeled and finely chopped
2 Turnips, peeled and finely chopped
6 Dry Red Chiles
8 C. Water
1 C. Olive Oil
16 Cloves of Garlic, peeled
12 Slices Bread
1 C. Tomatoes, peeled and strained
1 Lb. Monterey Jack or Longhorn Cheese, grated
8 Eggs
Salt to taste

Cook the vegetables with the meat in the water over low heat until the meat is very tender and the liquid reduces to about 4 C. Remove from the heat and set aside. Fry 12 slices of bread in olive oil, in which 16 cloves of garlic have been browned and removed. When the bread is brown, remove from the oil and drain on towels. In the oil sauté the onion and tomatoes. Add this sauce to the soup and simmer slowly for 5 minutes. In a glass casserole, arrange layers of fried bread, cut to size, and layers of cheese and then the soup, poured over the top. Break the eggs over the top and bake in a 400 degree oven until the whites set, about 6 to 8 minutes, or to your liking.

Caldo Encargado
RANCH FOREMAN'S SOUP

⅔ C. dried Peas
Water to cover peas
1¼ Lb. Marrow Bones
½ Lb. Mutton
1 Lb. Beef or Veal, for soup
1 Lb. Pork Loin
1 Chicken breast
2 Sm. Leeks
3 Sm. Turnips
6 Mint leaves
6 Cilantro leaves
6 Dry Red Chiles
6 Sm. Onions, with stems
2½ Tsp. Salt
3 Sm. Carrots
3 T. Cabbage, sliced
⅓ C. Rice

For the Garnish:
1 Avocado slice
1 Lemon wedge
Some Radishes, coarsely chopped
Some Fresh Green Chile, peeled and chopped
1 Sprig of Cilantro

Soak the peas overnight. Drain the peas, use the liquid and add additional water to make 5 quarts of soup stock. Add the marrow bones and boil 3 hours. Now add all the remaining ingredients and boil on a low flame for 4 hours longer. Remove the meat and bones, set aside for later use. Strain soup through double layer of cheesecloth. The resulting soup will be a little more than a quart. Place it in a double boiler until serving. Serve very hot. The cooked meats can be served as the meat dish for supper or can be chopped fine and added to the soup. Add the garnishes to the soup.

Sopa de Verduras
JULIENNE VEGETABLE SOUP

1 C. Each of the following: Carrots, Celery, Lettuce, Sorrel, Green Peas,
Snap Beans, Onion
Butter
1 Qt. Soup Stock

Cut all the vegetables, except the onion, in julienne strips. Sauté them in
butter, with a few slices of onion. Add 1 quart of boiling soup stock, gently boil
on a slow flame until the vegetables are tender and add some thin slices of
bread.

Sopa à la Catalana
CATALONIAN SOUP

This recipe is from Mrs. Juan Forster. Her husband, John Forster, owned
the Jurupa Rancho which is now Riverside County, California. It is one of several *ranchos* originally owned by the fabulous Lugo family, pioneers of Southern
California. The recipe appears as part of the Spanish Department in *How We
Cook in Los Angeles*, which was published in 1894.

1 Qt. Water
6 Oz. Beef
6 Oz. Mutton
¼ Chicken
½ C. Peas
Salt

When the water boils, put in the meat, chicken, and peas, with salt to
taste. Boil slowly, skimming carefully. When the meat is done, remove it. This
stock can be used for rice, noodles, or macaroni.

Sopa Española
GOVERNOR ALVARADO'S SOUP

4 Lbs. Veal, lean
½ Lb. Salt Pork, rind removed
2 Turnips, sliced
1 Lg. Carrot
1 Onion, sliced
1 Beet, sliced
4 T. Oatmeal
4 Oz. Cream
1 Tsp. Nutmeg
½ Tsp. Allspice
Salt and Pepper
Toast, cubed

Put the veal in a stock pot and cover with cold water. Let it simmer 4 hours. Skim to clarify. Mince the salt pork, sauté it to a light brown, and add it to the veal. One hour before serving, add the sliced turnips, onion, carrot, and beet. Simmer 40 minutes. Remove the vegetables and strain the broth through a colander back into the stock pot. Add the oatmeal and cook 20 minutes. Next add the cream and spices, salt and pepper. Pour into a soup tureen over diced, toasted bread. Serve the meat and vegetables on a separate platter or save for leftovers.

AT LEAST THEY HAD CHILES

Daniel Woods, author of Sixteen Months at the Gold Diggings, *complained of the dust storms and of the food and lodging in northern California—with one exception. "For his meals he must go to the fonda (inn), and order...a variety of soups, made hot with red pepper, and a slice of bread."*

Chile con Pollo Menudillos
CHICKEN GIBLET CHILE

4 Oz. each Giblets, Livers, and Hearts
Prepared Chile Sauce No. 1 or 2
Salt
Arroz Mexicana (Spanish Rice)
Queso Cotija or Parmesan Cheese

Cook chicken giblets, livers and hearts until tender in small amount water. Chop and add equal amount chile sauce No. 1 or 2, salt to taste, and cook for 5 minutes. Serve on Spanish Rice put in dish, sprinkle with parmesan cheese or a Mexican grated cheese called *cotija*.

Carne con Chile Blandido
MILD CHILE CON CARNE

2 C. Cooked Beef, chopped
½ C. Green Chile Pulp
½ C. Beef Suet
1 T. Lard
1 C. Tomatoes, chopped
1 Clove of Garlic, chopped
½ C. Onion, chopped

Put all ingredients in a Dutch oven and cook until thick. Serve with *frijoles*.

Pío Pico Carne con Chile
RED HOT CHILE CON CARNE

This recipe calls for ½ teaspoon of saffron, which would be about $32.00. Try maybe two pinches, if you aren't a millionaire. Nobody complains, and the Chile Con Carne tastes wonderful. Memorable, says Bertha Haffner-Ginger.

½ C. Salt Pork, chopped
½ C. Beef Suet
½ C. Onion, chopped
1 Tsp. Oregano
A pinch or two of Saffron
2 C. Cooked Beef, ground or chopped
2 C. Kidney Beans, cooked
2 C. Red Chile Pulp
2 C. Water
1 Bottle Beer
4 T. Chile Powder
Salt to taste

Sauté the salt pork with the beef suet, the chopped onion and fry until tender. Add the oregano, saffron and fry all together. Add the cooked beef, kidney beans, red chile pulp, water, beer, and chile powder, salt to taste. Cook 40 minutes. Serve with hot tortillas.

Variation: Use 1 T. Freshly ground toasted Cumin Seed.

Chile con Pollo
CHICKEN CHILE

Bertha Ginger lived in a time when chickens were probably better for stewing than now. This recipe will make a beautiful stock for use in soups and other recipes as well as a lovely low-fat chile con carne. Therefore, this recipe is as useful today as it was a century ago. Ask your butcher for a stewing hen 10 to 12 months old and 3 to 4 pounds in weight.

1 Stewing Chicken, 3-4 lbs., cut up
1-2 T. Flour
1 clove Garlic, minced
½ C. Onion, chopped
1 C. Green Chile Pulp
2 C. Chicken Stock
Salt
Spanish Rice

Cook the chicken in water to cover to make a chicken soup stock. When finished, save the chicken fat. Take the tender chicken and chop the meat into small pieces, heat some of the chicken fat skimmed from the stock, add the flour, garlic, and chopped onion. Then add the green chile pulp, stock, and salt. Add chopped chicken bits, stew for 10 minutes, serve on Spanish rice.

❖

AND WE THOUGHT MEXICAN FOOD WAS A NEW TREND

"There are firms in California putting up a specially prepared corn meal for tortillas. There are chile powders and canned red and green hot chiles; also the red sweet pepper, called pimiento, which makes it possible to cook Spanish dishes anywhere." – Bertha Ginger, 1914

❖

Chile con Carne No. 1

1 Lb. Beef, Veal, or Chicken
¼ C. Cilantro
8 Carrots
2 Celery Stalks
1 C. Onion, chopped
2-3 Bay Laurel leaves, crushed
3-4 C. Water
1 Bottle Beer (optional)
½ C. Red or Green Chile Pulp per pint of meat–broth mix
Frijoles Refritos (Refried Beans)

Cook the beef, veal, or chicken in a large dutch oven with the cilantro, peeled carrots, peeled celery, chopped onions, bay leaf, and 4 C. water or 3 C. water and 1 bottle of beer. Let it cook very slowly until tender, then cut meat into small pieces, strain the juice, and combine the meat and strained broth. Add to every pint of meat-broth mix, ½ C. chile pulp and 1 C. cooked and mashed frijoles. If too hot and spicy. add 1 C. tomatoes and cook few minutes longer to warm through.

Chile con Carne No. 2

May E. Southworth's *101 Mexican Dishes*, is probably the earliest English language cookbook devoted entirely to Mexican food. The Southworth's were some of the very first American pioneers, arriving in California in the 1840's, before the Gold Rush. Her *Chile Con Carne*, using pork, is a change from the ordinary.

5 Dry Red Chiles
Black Pepper, Garlic, and Salt to taste
2 Cloves
1 Tomato, roasted
1 Lb. Fresh Pork shoulder
Lard
Salt

Soak the chiles in hot water. Remove the stems, seeds and veins. Wash them well. Put in a mortar and pound to a pulp, adding the black pepper, garlic, cloves and grilled tomato. Set aside.

Cut the pork in chunks and parboil. Fry the chile sauce in hot lard; then add the meat, and some of the liquor in which it was boiled. Add a little salt. Cover and cook down until rather thick.

Carne con Chile Sepúlveda

Ana Bégué de Packman gives the following recipe and explanation for why the dish is called *Carne con Chile* and not *Chile con Carne*. "The meat being the main ingredient of the pot, and the chile only the sauce, it is insisted by the Californians that the meat be given the place of honor. From *Early California Hospitality.*

2 Lbs. Beef Chuck
1 Tsp. Salt
⅛ Tsp. Black Pepper
2 T. Fat from the Chuck

Sauce:
4 Oz. Dry Red Chiles
2 T. Fat (from Chuck)
2 T. Breadcrumbs, toasted
1 Clove of Garlic, mashed in salt
1 T. Vinegar
1 C. Black Olives

Cut the meat in chunks, removing as much fat and gristle as possible. Brown a little of the fat to render it, to grease the skillet. Use no fat if the meat is fatty already. Add the chunks of beef and season with the salt and pepper. Brown it well and set aside.

Stem and seed the chiles. Wipe them clean. Put them in a stew kettle and pour boiling water over them. Cook until the skin easily separates from the chile meat. Rub the chile-meat through a sieve. This should make about 1½ pints of red chile purée.

Heat enough of the fat to render 2 T., in an iron skillet. Add the toasted breadcrumbs and the garlic mashed in salt. Stir constantly until a light golden color. Pour in the chile purée, garlic, and the vinegar. Simmer 15 minutes. Add the meat. Cook 10 minutes longer. Serve, garnishing with the ripe olives.

Carne con Chile No. 2

Another Carne con Chile recipe comes from the Los Angeles Times' 1902 *Prize Cookbook, 453 Good Recipes by California House-keepers.*

1 Lb. Steak
1 small Clove of Garlic
1 Tsp. flour
7 Dried Red Chiles
Water
½ Tsp. Vinegar
Oregano or Marjoram

Take some nice, tender steak, cut in small pieces; cut about two inches long or whatever you care to cut it. Fry until done, with small piece of garlic about the size of a pea with 1 Tsp. flour. Mix well together until the meat is done.

Take about 7 good-sized dry red chiles, split and remove all the seeds; put in a pie plate in the oven to roast a few minutes; watch closely so they won't burn or scorch, for if they do, if will make the sauce taste bitter. When done, take out and cover with cold water, to soak about 10 minutes; then take your hands and mash well until the chiles are well ground; then take out all the skins, which leaves a thick sauce. Pour this over the meat and stir on low heat until it comes to a boil. Mix in ½ Tsp. vinegar when done cooking. Season to taste with oregano or marjoram.

Carne Ranchero
SPICY ROUND STEAK CHILE

From *Grandma Keeler's House Keeper* comes a most unusual chile con carne.

2 Lb. Round Steak
2 T. Olive Oil
6 Onions, chopped
1 Tsp. Garlic, minced
2 Green Chiles, chopped
2 Cans of Tomatoes (30 oz.), mashed with a spoon
2 Tsp. Thyme, ground
2 Tsp. Parsley, chopped
2 Tsp. Celery, minced
Cayenne Powder, to taste
Sapsago Cheese (no substitute or omit), grated

Chop the meat into bite-size pieces. Brown in 1 T. olive oil. Remove, add 1 T. olive oil, next add: the onions, garlic, chiles, and tomatoes, and fry until limp. Add the meat, season with the thyme, parsley, celery, and cayenne. Simmer 2 hours. Serve with *sapsago* cheese.

Dancing La Jota *rather than working*
Security Pacific Historical Photograph Collection, Los Angeles Public Library

CHAPTER 6

On The Hoof

Carne Asada con Salsas Champiñones

ELEGANT STEAK AND MUSHROOMS

Steak & Sauce:
8 Oz. of Top Sirloin Steak
2 T. Butter
1 T. Olive Oil
1 T. Onion, minced
1 Clove of Garlic
1 T. Cilantro or Parsley
1 T. Green Bell Pepper, minced
2 T. Chile Pulp (Green or Red)
1 T. Flour
2 C. Fresh Tomatoes, chopped

Garnish:
2 T. Butter
4 Oz. Mushrooms
Serranos Chile Strips (1 or 2)
2 Oz. Ripe Olives
Salt to taste
Cilantro
Longhorn Cheese (optional)

Select a tender steak, then make ready a sauce as follows: Melt butter and olive oil together. Add the minced onion and garlic and brown them well. Add the cilantro, bell pepper and chile pulp, to heat through, but stir constantly to keep from scorching the cilantro. Add 1 T. flour and brown, add 2 C. fresh chopped tomatoes, cook 5 minutes. Strain the sauce.

Heat a skillet for the steak. Slightly grease the very hot skillet with olive oil. Heat until almost smoking. Sear steak on both sides, turning until cooked as desired. While steak is cooking, melt the butter and sauté the mushrooms, chile serrano strips and ripe olives in butter, leave in pan until ready for garnishing. Pour previously made sauce over hot steak. Garnish with sautéed mushrooms, chile serrano strips, and ripe olives. Sprinkle with salt and garnish with sprigs of cilantro.

Variation: If cheese is liked, sprinkle grated longhorn cheese over steak and sauce, melt in oven, serve hot, or use Prepared Spanish Sauce.

Carne Asada Sencilla
SIMPLE STEAK

2 Lbs. Round Steak
Suet, chopped
Water
Salt
Pepper
1 C. Onion, chopped
1 T. Lard or Butter
1 T. Flour
1 16 Oz. Can Tomatoes
1 Tsp. Oregano
2 T. Green Chile Pulp
Longhorn Cheese

Select 2 pounds upper round steak, sear on hot skillet on both sides till crust is formed; then add ½ C. chopped suet, ½ C. hot water, cover; bring to boil then simmer 30 minutes, add salt and pepper.

Fry the chopped onions in lard or butter until slightly brown; add 1 T. flour, the tomatoes, oregano, green chile pulp and heat through. Spread over the steak, cover, and cook 20 minutes longer. Place on serving dish, sprinkle with cheese, set in oven to melt cheese and serve hot.

Bistec Flanco Gordo
SPANISH FLANK STEAK

1½ Lb. Flank Steak
4 Oz. Flour
Salt
2 Oz. Chile Powder
3 T. Lard or Suet, melted
8 Oz. Bread Crumbs
2 C. Tomatoes, chopped
4 T. Chile Pulp (Red or Green)
2 T. Onion, chopped
1 T. Oregano
3 Bay Leaves, crumbled
Salt

Have the butcher criss-cross or tenderize a flank steak. Rub into it the flour, seasoned with salt and chile powder, spread with 2 T. lard or melted suet. Make a filling of bread crumbs, 1 C. tomato, chile pulp, onion, oregano, bay leaf, and salt. Place on the steak and roll up and tie. Put 1 T. lard, 1 C. tomato, a little salt on top, to cover the steak then bake 2 or 3 hours slowly, in a 325 degree oven.

❁

BUT WAS THERE A TENDERLOIN *RANCHO?*

In the San Francisco area, notwithstanding the claims of the mission-aries that the Church owned all the land from one mission to another, there were, in 1830, about fifty ranchos in possession of private individuals. They included families with names such as: Argüello, Arellanes, Castro, Estudillo, Vallejo, Peralta, after which many streets and towns are named. They were some of the original Californios.

❁

Chuleta Chula California

CALIFORNIO PORK TENDERLOIN CUTLETS

1 Lb. Pork Tenderloin, cut into cutlets
6 T. Flour
2 Tsp. Salt
Pepper
2 T. Chile Powder
Bacon Fat
Toast Triangles
Lettuce
2 Fresh Tomatoes
2 C. Rice, cooked
Cilantro
Butter (optional)

Pound the tenderloins out flat and cover with flour, seasoned with salt, pepper, and chile powder. Fry until brown in hot bacon fat. Place triangles of toast in center of platter, arrange the cutlets to stand around the toast. Put lettuce cups around outside of cutlets and fill each with ½ peeled tomato, sprinkled with cooked rice and chopped cilantro, a little salt and chile powder.

Variation: Stuff whole tomatoes with a mixture of cooked chopped meat and rice, seasoned with salt, chile powder, onion and top with butter. Bake until brown on top. Garnish with cilantro and set twig of cilantro in center of toast.

CALIFORNIO MEAT PATTIES

½ Lb. Ground Pork
½ Lb. Ground Beef
1 C. Bread
1 Bottle of Beer
1 Egg, beaten
¼ C. Onion, minced
1 Tsp. Salt
1 T. Green Chile Pulp
1 C. Red Chile Sauce #1

Mix the ground pork and beef together, add the bread, wetted with some beer. Add the egg, onion, salt, green chile pulp, mix and make into patties one inch thick. Put 1 C. prepared red sauce in pan and heat, place meat in sauce, cover, simmer till done. Serve with mashed potatoes and a green vegetable.

AT THAT PRICE, GIVE ME FIVE HEAD OF CATTLE

The old open-air markets of San Francisco had food serving counters where a meal could be had for only 25 cents. And what a meal! If one ordered steak, along with it came shrimp, crab legs, or perhaps pigs' feet. A loaf or half a loaf of French bread was thrown in for good measure. Dressed beef was 5 cents a pound.

Albondigas Deliciosas
DELICIOUS MEATBALLS

1 Lb. of Beef, Veal or Chicken
½ C. Mushrooms, chopped
2 T. Butter
1 C. Bread Crumbs
1 Tsp. Onion juice
Bechamel Sauce (see recipe)
Salt
1 T. Olive Oil
1 T. Butter
6 Olives, chopped
1 T. Onion, chopped
1 T. Flour
1 T. Butter
1 T. Olive Oil
Salt
Paprika
1 C. Canned or Fresh Tomatoes, chopped
1 C. Green Chile Pulp
Cilantro

Use finely ground beef, veal, or chicken, raw or cooked. Brown ¼ C. chopped mushrooms in 1 T. butter. To each C. of ground meat, add ½ C. wet bread crumbs and chopped mushrooms, 1 Tsp. onion juice, ¼ C. Bechamel Sauce and salt to taste. Make into round flat patties; fry in small amount of olive oil and butter, until browned.

Make a sauce of 6 chopped olives, remaining ¼ C. mushrooms, 1 T. onion, 1 T. flour, 1 T. each of olive oil and butter. Add salt and paprika, and 1 C. fresh or canned tomatoes, and green chile pulp, heat through, and pour around meat cakes. Sprinkle with chopped cilantro and serve.

Pulchero Grueso
STANDING GREATER PART OF BEEF

May Southworth's *One Hundred & One Mexican Dishes* is gourmet cooking at its finest, as this recipe attests. This recipe is vaguely reminiscent of Brazil's *Feijoada*, except for the omission of black beans.

3 Lbs. of Beef
1 Pig's foot
½ Lb. Ham
Giblets of a chicken or fowl
1 Green Chile, chopped fine
Water
1 Slice of Pumpkin, seeds removed
½ Sm. Cabbage
1 Lg. Carrot
Bunch of Herbs (Oregano, Basil, Marjoram, Mint, as you like it)
2 Lg. Onions, chopped
Handful or two of Macaroni
6-8 Oz. Chorizo (casings removed)
Cornstarch

Chop the beef, pig's foot, ham, giblets, and chile. Simmer for 2 hours, adding water as necessary to prevent scorching. Add the pumpkin slice, cabbage, carrot, herbs, onion, and macaroni. Cook 1 hour longer, then add the chorizo and boil until done. Strain the meat and vegetables, thicken the liquor to make a gravy (1 T. cornstarch mixed in water). Serve the meat and vegetables on separate platters.

Guisado de Res
SPANISH BEEF STEW

1 Lb. Beef or Veal Stew Meat
Beef Suet
½ C. Onion, chopped
4 C. Tomatoes
1 Bay Laurel Leaf
½ Clove of Garlic
1 Egg, beaten with ½ Tsp. of water
1 Tsp. Mint Leaves
2 T. Minced Bell Pepper
½ Tsp. Oregano
1 Tsp. Salt
1 T. Butter
3 T. Corn Masa Flour

Mix the mint leaves, bell pepper, oregano, salt and butter together to a batter-like consistency. Set aside to thicken.

Cut the beef or veal in small two inch pieces, flour them thickly in the corn masa. Dip them in the beaten egg and next coat them in the batter. Brown them in hot suet. To a pot add the onions, garlic, bay leaf and tomatoes and bring to a boil. Then add the browned meat. Lower to a simmer on the stovetop until done. Serve with Prepared Spanish Sauce.

Salpicón Español
SPANISH HASH

Use an eight-inch baking dish for this recipe.

3 Lbs. Russet Potatoes
Milk
Salt
Pepper
1 Lb. Leftover Meat, Fish, Fowl
1¼ C. Onion, sliced
1 T. Olive Oil
1 Fresh Green New Mexican Chile, chopped
1 Fresh Red Bell Pepper, chopped
Cilantro
Chile Pulp
Flour
½ C. Tomatoes (canned)
Bread Crumbs
Longhorn or Monterey Jack Cheese

Peel and quarter baking potatoes and boil in salted water, about 25 minutes. Drain. Put potatoes in a large bowl and coarsely mash with fork. Make a well in the center and add a little milk. Beat milk into potatoes with a fork. Add more milk until the correct consistency is obtained. Cautiously add salt and pepper tasting all the time. Set aside.

Reheat enough meat, fowl or fish to make a layer for the baking dish. Do this by putting a little oil in a skillet, brown ¼ C. onions. Add meats and season with salt and pepper. Heat through. Remove from skillet and set aside.

Prepare a top layer by sautéing in the same skillet the following: 1 T. oil, 1 C. sliced onions, the green chile, and the bell pepper, chopped nicely. Next, add 1 T. chopped cilantro, 1 T. chile pulp, salt and 1 T. flour. Add ½ C. canned tomatoes and simmer until the sauce thickens.

Into the baking dish, add a layer of the potatoes about 1 inch thick, then the meat layer, then pour the sauce over the meat. Then sprinkle a mixture of bread crumbs and cheese and bake for 40 minutes in a 325 degree oven until the cheese browns a little.

Salpicón Español Adobado

SPANISH CURRY HASH

2 T. Butter
3 T. Onion, chopped
1 C. Ground Beef, Pork, or Veal
1 C. Tomatoes, chopped
10 Olives, sliced
1 T. Worcestershire Sauce
1 Green Bell Pepper, chopped
¼ Tsp. Curry Powder
1 T. Flour
1 C. Meat Stock or Water
Salt
4 C. Rice, cooked
Butter
Cilantro
2 Hard Boiled Eggs

Brown in 2 T. butter the chopped onion, ground meat, canned tomatoes, olives, Worcestershire sauce, green pepper, curry powder, and flour. Next add 1 C. any meat stock or hot water. Cook until thickened. Salt to taste. In a baking dish, alternate layers of the meat and cooked rice. Pour a little melted butter over top and bake in a 325 degree oven for 1 hour. Garnish with cilantro and slices of hard cooked egg.

Guisado de Conejo
SPANISH STEWED RABBIT

The gravy is delicious.

1 Young Rabbit, cut up
Corn Masa
Flour
Salt
Chile Powder
Oil
Prepared Spanish Sauce
Hot Water
½ C. Raisins, soaked in wine
Toast Triangles
Mint Leaves

Roll the rabbit pieces in a mixture of corn masa, flour, salt, and chile powder. Fry in hot oil until brown. Cover with Spanish sauce, a little hot water, and add the wine-soaked raisins. Stew 10 minutes, garnish with toast and mint.

Bistec
BEEFSTEAK

2 Lbs. Round Steak (2 inches thick)
1 C. Hot Water
Salt and Pepper
1 Lb. Onions, thin sliced
4 Green Chiles, chopped fine
8 Oz. Stewed Tomatoes

Put the steak in a baking dish and add hot water. Place in a 350 degree oven for 30 minutes. Baste often. Remove, sprinkle with salt and pepper to taste and cover with the sliced onions and chiles. Bake 15 minutes longer. Remove and cover with the tomatoes, return to oven for 20 minutes longer. To serve, put meat and vegetables on a heated platter and pour gravy around the meat.

Asado Español Giro
ROLLED SPANISH STEAK

2 Lb. thick Sirloin Steak
2 Green Chiles, chopped fine
3 Med. Onion, chopped fine
3 Sm. Tomatoes, peeled and chopped fine
3 Stalks Celery, peeled and chopped fine
1 Sprig Parsley
1 C. Breadcrumbs
1 Lg. Egg, beaten
1 T. Butter, melted
Flour
Salt and Pepper to taste
Olives for garnish
Celery Leaves for garnish

Remove the fat from a thick Sirloin Steak. Pound it a little to tenderize and enlarge it. Thoroughly mix the chiles, onion, tomatoes, celery stalks, and parsley with the breadcrumbs. Add the lightly beaten egg to moisten enough and shape into a loaf. Mound the loaf over the steak. Roll the steak up like a jelly roll. Tie it to hold the shape. Put the trussed steak into a baking pan, with some hot water. Add a walnut-sized piece of butter for basting. Sprinkle the top of the meat with a little flour and dust with salt and pepper. Put in a 350 degree oven and bake. Baste often, until done. Remove from oven. Remove meat and put onto serving platter. Season the juice with the herbs and spices you like (oregano and chile powder) and a little flour to thicken, stirring constantly to prevent lumping. Cut the roast into thick slices and garnish with the gravy, olives, and celery leaves.

Tenera Enrollarse Encantado

VEAL BRISKET STUFFED A LA CALIFORNIO

1 Med. Onion, chopped
4 T. Butter
2 C. Bread crumbs
1 C. Milk
4 T. Parsley, chopped
2 Green Chiles, minced
1 Lb. Chorizo
4-5 Lb. Veal brisket

In a sauté pan, brown the onion in 2 T. butter. Dip the bread crumbs in the milk, remove and let drain a little. Add the drained bread crumbs, parsley, and minced chiles to the onion and heat through. Add the chorizo and stir to mix. Stuff the brisket with the mixture and sew it up. Put the loaf in a baking dish with 1 C. of hot water. Rub 2 T. butter over the loaf. Put in a preheated 350 degree oven for 2 hours, basting at intervals.

Para Masa Rellenos

MEAT DUMPLINGS

1 Lb. Beef, Pork, or Chicken, ground
½ C. Bacon, chopped
1 C. Tomatoes
2 Tsp. Salt
2 T. Chile Powder
Corn Masa
Water
3 T. Tomatoes, chopped
Lard

Mix 2 C. meat (raw or cooked), add chopped bacon, 2 Tsp. salt, and 2 T. chile powder. Mix to a thick dough with corn masa to make into balls the size of walnuts. Drop in salted, boiling water with the tomatoes, add a little lard and cook 20 minutes. Add corn masa to thicken water when meat is done.

Chonzo

1 Lb. Pork Shoulder, chopped
1 Lb. Beef, rump, chopped
2 Cloves Garlic, mashed
1 Tsp. Chile Powder
⅓ Tsp. Cloves, ground
1 Tsp. Pepper
1 Tsp. Oregano
Salt to taste
4 Oz. Port wine
2 T. Olive Oil
2 Eggs, fresh
2 T. Water

Chop the meat into small pieces. Mash the garlic with a little salt. In a mixing bowl, add the meat, mashed garlic, chile powder, cloves, pepper, oregano, a little more salt, and the wine. Set aside.

In a large skillet, heat the olive oil, when hot add the meat and seasoning mixture and sauté. When ready, break the eggs in a small mixing bowl, add 2 T. water, beat quickly and scramble the eggs and seasoned meat together.

NOW THEY GO TO McDONALD'S

The Californio's work day consisted of a dawn breakfast of little more than coffee and a roll. About mid-morning, breakfast, called the almuerzo, would be served. American farmers still follow this practice, eating a huge lunch before returning to work afterwards. Dinner is for these people a lighter affair.

Lengua de Vaca Cocida
SAVORY TONGUE

Salt
Water
1 Beef Tongue
12 Chiles Anchos
1 Tsp. Summer Savory, ground
2 Tsp. Onion, finely chopped
½ C. Olive Oil
2 Lemons
Wine Vinegar
12 Oz. bottled Olives, finely chopped

Dissolve ½ C. salt in enough hot water to cover the tongue. Cook until just done, about 1 hour and 20 minutes. Allow to cool in the stock. Remove the skin and slice the tongue thin. Put the tongue back in the stock to cool completely.

While the tongue is cooking put the 12 anchos in a pot of water with 2 Tsp. salt to boil. Boil until they are limp, approximately 30 minutes. Remove, allow to cool in their stock. When cool enough to work, skin them, and remove the stem, seeds and veins. Or cut them lengthwise, flatten with meat side up, scrape the meat out and discard the skin, seed and stem. Use some of the cooking liquid to make a paste or thick gravy. Add the savory, chopped onion, salt, and ½ C. olive oil. Squeeze the lemons into a measuring cup, then fill with wine vinegar to 1 C. total. Add this to the sauce by spoonfuls, and a bottle of olives, chopped fine. Heat the sauce through and pour over the tongue as it is served.

Patitas con Cacahuate
Pigs Feet in Peanuts

2 Pig's feet
2 Oz. White Vinegar
6-8 New Potatoes, peeled and quartered
1 C. Peanuts, roasted
Olive Oil
Allspice
Salt

Wash the pig's feet thoroughly. In a kettle of water, add some vinegar to acidulate. Bring the trotters to a boil and then lower to a simmer for 2 to 2½ hours. Allow to cool in the liquor.

Parboil the peeled and quartered potatoes. Set aside until the pig's feet are ready. Chop ½ C. of the peanuts and mix with the remainder of the peanuts. Remove the pig's feet and dry. Sauté the potatoes, peanuts, and the pigs' feet in hot olive oil. Season with allspice and salt to taste. Stir constantly so as to brown on all sides. Sauté 10 minutes.

The First Commerical Farmers

The first commercial scale farming in California was started by Isaac Lankershim and Isaac Newton Van Nuys in 1876. The eastern part of the San Fernando Valley was sown with wheat. It was so successful that the crops were exported. This was about twenty-five years before the Owens Valley water was brought to Los Angeles for crop irrigation.

Puerco en Estofado
STUFFED PORK CHOPS

4 T. Olive Oil
1 T. White wine vinegar
1 T. Worcestershire Sauce
Dash Cloves, powdered
Salt and pepper to taste
1 Lb. Pork Chops, de-boned and chopped
Gizzards and livers of 2 chickens
1 Oz. Ginger, fresh, peeled and cut julienne
3 Celery Stalks, peeled and chopped
½ C. boiling Water
1 C. Bean Sprouts
1 C. Mushrooms, bottled

Mix the olive oil, vinegar, Worcestershire sauce, cloves, salt and pepper. Set aside to blend. Sauté the chopped pork; add the gizzards and livers, the ginger and celery. Add the oil and spice mixture a spoonful at a time to the meats. When all the oil is added, add ½ C. boiling water and cook until nearly done, about 30 minutes. Next, add 1 C. bean sprouts and 1 C. mushrooms. Stir well and serve.

Tia Juana
Aunty Juanita's Sausages

1 Lb. Chorizo, formed into meatballs
1 Clove of Garlic, minced
1 Med. Onion, chopped
15 Oz. can of Tomatoes
1 Green Chile, chopped
1 Lb. Tripe, preferably Moreno
Flour
Butter
Salt

Make the chorizo into balls. 1 lb. of chorizo should make 12 to 16 meatballs. Fry the garlic and onion and the meatballs together. When the meat begins to brown, add the tomatoes and the chile. Meanwhile, scald 1 lb. of tripe, scrape it free of fat and gristle and cut it into rectangles about 2 inches by 5 inches. Roll them up and tie with a string. Dredge the rolls in flour and brown them golden in butter. Remove to a hot platter. Lift the sausages from the sauce and heap in the center of the tripe. Strain the sauce, adjust the salt, reheat and pour over all.

Santa Barbara Mission photographed in the moonlight
Paul Elder Publishing, Circa 1911

CHAPTER 7

Fish

Guisado de Pescado
SPANISH FISH STEW

1 Lb. White Fish or Red Snapper
Salt
Corn Masa
Bacon Fat
Olive Oil
½ C. Onion, sliced
Tomatoes (Canned only)
2 T. Chile Pulp
Salt to taste
Saffron
Oregano
New Potatoes, quartered and cooked
Cilantro, chopped

Cut the fish in ¾ inch pieces, salt and roll in corn masa. Heat 1 T. bacon fat and 1 T. of olive oil in a skillet. Add ½ C. sliced onion, fry till brown, add fish and fry till brown. Add enough tomato to barely cover the fish. Add the chile pulp, salt to taste, a pinch of saffron and oregano. Cook a few minutes. Serve on platter. Garnish with new potato sprinkled with chopped cilantro.

BEGINNINGS OF THE BAY AREA

On June 20, 1820, Don Pablo Vicente de Sola, Governor of California, granted to Sergeant Luis Peralta land to be known as Rancho San Antonio. It consisted of eleven leagues or 48,825 acres. Four leagues would have been for crops and seven used for cattle and living area. That area now comprises the towns of Oakland, Alameda and Berkeley. Peralta Boulevard in Alameda County remembers his name and heirs.

Pescado al Horno

SPANISH BAKED FISH

3 C. Bread Crumbs
1 C. Tomatoes (canned)
1 T. Onion, minced
1 T. Cilantro
2 T. Butter
10 Olives, sliced
½ C. Seedless Raisins
2 to 3 Lb. Fish (Red Snapper), whole but scaled and cleaned
Olive oil
Prepared Spanish Sauce
Lemon & Cilantro for garnish

In a bowl, make a filling of bread crumbs wetted with canned tomatoes liquid. Next add the minced onion, chopped cilantro, ½ C. tomato pulp, 2 T. melted butter, ten sliced olives, and ½ C. seedless raisins. Use mixture to fill the fish and sew it up. Place the fish in a large frying pan in olive oil and fry until golden. When done, remove carefully to hot platter and peel off skin. Pour hot Prepared Spanish sauce over fish. Garnish with lemon and cilantro.

Variation: Soak the bread crumbs and raisins in a good wine or strong beer. Let raisins soak at least 20 minutes before soaking bread crumbs.

Pescado Frito
MONTEREY FRIED FISH

1 Lb. Barracuda fillets or any other tender fish
Salt
1 T. Onion, minced
1 T. Olive Oil
1 T. Flour
1 C. Tomatoes, chopped
2 T. Red or Green Chile Pulp
Salt
1 Egg, beaten
Flour
Milk
Salt
Olive oil

Garnish:
Green Bell Pepper, Lemon, and Cilantro

Salt the barracuda, let drain in colander for twenty minutes. While it is draining, make a sauce by browning the onion in the olive oil, adding a tablespoon of flour and browning, then the tomatoes, red or green chile pulp and salt, cook until it is like a gravy.

Next make a batter of egg, flour, milk and salt. Once the fish has dried, dip it in the batter. Fry fish till browned in deep, hot, olive oil, enough to cover fish. Remove to a platter. Pour sauce across center of fish, allowing brown crisp ends to show. Garnish with slices of sweet green pepper, lemon, and cilantro.

Pescado Estofado
CALIFORNIO FISH STEW

2 Lb. Barracuda, Sea Bass or Rock Cod
1 Lg. Onion
2 T. Olive Oil, Bacon fat or Salt Pork
1 C. Tomatoes
2 Green Chiles, roasted, peeled, chopped
1 C. Hot Water
1 T. Flour, to thicken
1 T. Oregano
Pinch of Saffron
Salt and Pepper to taste

Garnish:
Buttered Toast Triangles, Cilantro

Skin and bone the fish and cut it into 4 pieces. Slice the onion thin. In a stew pot, heat the olive oil or other fat and lightly brown the onion. Add the tomatoes, chile, flour and hot water, then bring to a boil, lower heat and simmer 20 minutes.

Next, add the fish. If necessary, add enough boiling water to just cover the fish. Let simmer 20 minutes until the fish is tender. Season the broth with 1 T. oregano, a good pinch of Saffron and salt and pepper. Serve on a platter garnished with buttered toast triangles. Sprinkle 1 T. minced cilantro over the fish.

❧

THE BEGINNINGS OF SAN FRANCISCO CUISINE

Good food and wine came early to California. Diego de Borica, commandant of the Presidio of San Francisco from 1794 to 1800, expressed the following sentiment about San Francisco:
"The fine climate, the abundance of wine of the Rhine, of Madeira, and of Oporto, of the good bread, beef, fish and other good eatables..."

❧

Salmón Californio
SALMON WITH SALSA CALIFORNIA

1 Lb. Salmon, cleaned, poached, or from a can
Cilantro for garnish

Sauce:
1 Red Chile, roasted, peeled and chopped
1 Green Chile, roasted, peeled and chopped
1 Clove of Garlic, chopped
1 Sm. Onion, chopped
1 T. Butter
Juice from 1 qt. of Tomatoes, strained
1 T. Flour
½ Tsp. Salt
½ Tsp. Celery Salt
1 Tsp. Worcestershire Sauce or Ketchup

For the Salmon:
Put the salmon in a baking dish and bake in a 300 degree oven for 20 minutes. Remove and garnish with cilantro. Pour the sauce on plates, cut up or break up the salmon to top and garnish with chopped cilantro.

For the sauce:
Sauté the chiles, garlic, and onion in the butter for 10 minutes. In a pot, warm the strained tomato juice and blend in the flour slowly to insure a smooth consistency. Add to the above, cooking for 15 minutes longer. Next add the salt, celery salt, and Worcestershire sauce. Stir this constantly while cooking. Heat to thicken slightly. This should make enough sauce for 2 meals and is good for any meat dish.

Pescado en Caracol al Horno
BAKED FISH IN SHELLS

Ask the fish monger for some abalone shells or any that are not too dear. Or serve oysters and save the shells for another day.

For the fish boil:
3 Lb. Ocean fish: snapper, tuna, swordfish, et cetera
½ Lemon, sliced
3 Sm. Onions, sliced
2 Jalapeño Chiles, pickled, sliced in strips
2 Cloves, whole
1 Bay Laurel Leaf

For the forcemeat:
½ C. Olive Oil
½ C. Onions, minced
1 Clove Garlic, chopped
1 C. Tomato purée or sauce
1 Tsp. Parsley, minced
½ C. Bread crumbs, toasted
Salt and Pepper to taste
Butter
Liquid Hot Sauce

Place the fish in a quart of water acidulated with lemon. Add the onions, jalapeños, cloves, and bay laurel leaf. Bring to a boil for 10 minutes. Allow the fish to cool in the broth.

Heat a non-stick skillet, add the oil, onions and garlic. Brown them slightly, add the tomato purée, 3 T. fish broth and the parsley. Bring to a simmer.

Prepare the fish as follows. Bone and shred the fish, mix the sauce and fish meat together. Butter the shells and fill them with the fish-sauce mixture. Sprinkle toasted breadcrumbs on top, dot with butter and a dash of liquid hot sauce. Bake to a light brown in a 300 degree oven. Salt and pepper to taste.

Variation: Use capers in place of the pickled peppers.

Ostras Angelinos
LOS ANGELES OYSTERS

6 Oysters per person, shucked
1 Strip Bacon per oyster
Salt
Chile powder
Toast

Cook a slice of bacon for each oyster. Do not fry the bacon crisp. Wrap each oyster in a thin slice of bacon, securing with a toothpick. Sprinkle with salt and chile powder. Broil and serve on toast.

Trucha Jurupa
TROUT À LA CASCARA

Mrs. Juan Forster, an early Californio, was extraordinarily fond of the following; you will love it too.

1 Rainbow Trout
Salt
Water
1 T. Olive Oil
1 T. Flour
1 Med. Onion, peeled, left whole
1 Head of Garlic
1 Tsp. Parsley
Peppermint, to taste
Cloves, to taste
Thyme Sprig, fresh, whole
Basil, to taste

Clean the trout. Cover it with salt for 1 hour. Wash the salt off and bring a pot of water to the boil quickly. Hold the boil, with sufficient water to cover the trout, and add all the remaining ingredients. Cook 20 minutes. Start testing at 15 minutes. When done, remove the trout and serve on warmed plates.

Pescado Embarcadero

FISH AT THE WHARF

4-6 Lb. Red Snapper, scaled and cleaned
Salt
Pepper
Oregano
1 C. White Wine
1 C. Olive Oil
½ C. Wine Vinegar
1 Qt. Stuffed Green Olives
1 Can Peas, drained
1 Lb. String Beans, cooked
2 Pickled Onions, sliced
1 Can Asparagus tips
2 Eggs, hard boiled, chopped
Parsley, chopped

Rub the fish with salt, pepper, and oregano. Put the fish in a baking dish in a 350 degree oven for 15 minutes, then add the wine. Continue to bake at 300 degrees until thoroughly cooked. Time will depend on size of fish. Remove from the oven and allow to cool thoroughly. Transfer to a large serving platter.

In a bowl, mix the oil, vinegar, salt, pepper, and oregano. When well blended add the stuffed olives, peas, string beans, pickled onions, and asparagus tips. Mix well and stuff the center of the fish, putting the balance around the sides and on top of the fish. Garnish with chopped hard boiled eggs and parsley.

Salmón Estilo Español
SALMON MONTEREY

In the same school as the above is Mrs. Sepúlveda de Mott's salmon.

4 C. Chicken Stock or fish stock
2 Leeks, cleaned and thick sliced per diner
2 Salmon steaks or fillets
A few Peppercorns
Parsley to garnish

Into a boiling stock, add the leeks, the salmon, and a few peppercorns. Cook for 20 minutes, testing after 12 to 15 minutes. When ready to serve, using a strainer, remove the leeks. Put the fish on a serving platter and put the leeks around the edge of the fish. Garnish with a little chopped parsley.

Pescado Asado Ahumado con Laurel
GRILLED FISH SMOKED WITH BAY LEAVES

1 Fish (2 to 3 lbs.)
Salt
Pepper
Lemon Juice
Olive Oil
Bay Laurel Leaves, soaked in wine, water, or beer
Scallions
Parsley

Clean the fish and wipe it dry. Make a grill sauce of salt, pepper, lemon juice, and olive oil. Brush the fish with the sauce. Put it on the grill and throw some soaked bay laurel leaves under the fish from time to time so that the fish receives the smoke. Turn the fish frequently, brushing with the grill sauce, until it is golden. Serve with chopped whites of scallions and minced parsley. Alternatively, marinate scallions in a little lemon juice for 10 to 20 minutes and serve with the minced parsley over the fish.

Truchas Rellenas y Empapeladas
STUFFED TROUT IN PARCHMENT

The ingredient list is for each fish and diner. Feel free to vary the proportions of the stuffing to individual taste. Proportions given are approximate.

1 Trout, scaled and cleaned
Parchment
Butter or olive oil

Stuffing:
1 Oz. Almonds, ground
1 Oz. Olives, Black or Green, pitted and minced
½ Tsp. Green Chiles, roasted, peeled seeded and minced
¼ Med. Onion, finely chopped
1 T. Parsley, chopped
Salt
Black Pepper
Oregano
Capers
Oil
Wine Vinegar

Scale and clean the trout, one per diner. Set them aside in the refrigerator. A few minutes before the fish are to be stuffed, rub the parchment with butter or olive oil. Set them aside.

Mix all the stuffing ingredients and stuff the fish. When they are all stuffed, cover them with seasoned bread crumbs. Drizzle olive oil all over and wrap the fish in the parchment. Close with toothpicks, if necessary. Put them on the grill to roast, turning carefully. If parchment paper is unavailable, lightly oiled white paper bags from the bakery will do. The rule of thumb is 10 minutes per inch of fish, measured at the thickest part.

Variation: Bake the trout in butter without the parchment bag.

CHAPTER 8

Chicken Dishes

Guisado de Pollo

CHICKEN STEW

1 Roaster Chicken, cut up
Salt
Flour
Olive Oil
1 T. Butter
½ C. Onion, sliced
1 Clove of Garlic, chopped
1 Tsp. Cilantro
2 T. Flour
2 C. Tomatoes, chopped
2 T. Chile Pulp
1 Tsp. Sugar
Toast
Green Peas

Dredge the chicken in salt and flour, brown in a small amount of olive oil. Keep hot in oven, once fried. Then add the following ingredients: butter, to the oil left in frying pan, onions, garlic, cilantro, flour, and brown all together. Then add the chopped tomatoes, chile pulp and 1 Tsp. sugar; cook until sauce thickens and pour over chicken. Garnish with buttered toast and green peas.

❖

THE END OF THE COUNTRY LIFESTYLE

In 1889, the Los Angeles City Council outlawed grazing livestock and chickens in the city, which stretched from the Plaza south about as far as Second Street in those days.

❖

Pollo Tapando
Stuffed Chicken

1 Chicken (2-3 Lbs.)
Cooking Oil
2 C. Bread Crumbs
3 T. Green Bell Pepper Pulp
1 C. Tomatoes
2 T. Onion, chopped
½ C. Claret
2 T. Sugar
½ C. Onions, sliced
½ C. Seedless Raisins
1 Tsp. White Pepper
Salt
8 Oz. Mushrooms
Olive oil

Brown a fat, tender frying chicken in a small amount of oil by turning over and over for a few minutes. Make a dressing of the remaining ingredients, except the mushrooms and olive oil. Stuff the chicken with the dressing and bake in a covered pan for 1 hour in a medium oven.

Make gravy of drippings by adding flour, mushroom sauce, and hot water. Pour over chicken.

To make Mushroom Sauce:
Clean the mushrooms, cut off stem end, discard. Chop remaining mushrooms into medium dice. Sauté in hot butter or olive oil.

Pollo al Horno en Caserola

BAKED CHICKEN CASSEROLE

Salt
1 Chicken (2-3 lbs.)
1 White Onion, sliced
Butter
Flour
Hot water
1 Tsp. Oregano
1 6 to 8 oz. can Mushrooms
12 Olives, sliced
2 T. Chile Sauce No. 2
1 Chile Serrano, minced
2 C. Tomatoes, chopped
1 T. Butter
1 T. Flour
Salt
1 C. Cream
Buttered Toast Triangles
Dry Sack or other Good Quality Sherry

Salt a tender chicken, rub it inside and out with thick slice of onion. Then rub with butter and flour it. Put the chicken in a large casserole. Pour in the bottom 1 C. hot water and the oregano. Then add the can of mushrooms, the olives, chile sauce, chile serrano, tomatoes, butter, and 1 T. flour to thicken. Salt to taste, cover and simmer 45 minutes. Add the 1 C. of cream and cook 15 minutes longer. Dip buttered toast in sherry—enough toast for each guest. Do not use cooking sherry. Lay on top of chicken, cover, let it stand a few minutes. Serve from the casserole.

Aderezo para Pavo o Pollo
DRESSING FOR CHICKEN OR TURKEY

1 C. Chicken or Turkey Stock
1 Lb. Corn Meal
½ C. Chestnuts, roasted and chopped
1 T. Butter
1 Hardboiled Egg, minced
1 Tsp. Black Pepper
3 T. Red Chile Pulp
¼ C. Onion, minced
1 Heaping T. Chopped Cilantro
1 Egg, whisked lightly
Salt to taste
Chile Sauce No. 2

In a large bowl, mix together all the ingredients except the chile sauce. Stuff a turkey or chicken and bake. Make the usual dressing of the drippings, add prepared chile sauce No. 2, and serve on the dressing.

Pollo en Vino
CHICKEN IN WINE

Olive oil
1 chicken, cut up
3 Green Chiles, roasted, peeled, chopped
1 Lg. Onion, chopped
15 Oz. can Tomatoes, chopped
1 C. Claret
3 T. Sugar
1 Handful of Raisins
3-6 whole Cloves
Salt and Pepper to taste
Water
2 T. Flour

Heat the oil in a large dutch oven. Put in the chicken, turning several times to brown, then add the chiles, onion and tomatoes. Stir for 4 minutes. Add the wine, sugar, raisins, cloves, salt, and freshly ground black pepper. Stir together well, add 1 quart of water. Cover with a tight fitting lid. Simmer 60 minutes or until chicken is tender. Remove the chicken and stir in 2 T. flour to thicken for gravy.

123

Estofado de Pollo
CHICKEN FRICASSEE

1 4-lb. Chicken
Flour
Olive oil
3 T. Worcestershire Sauce
Salt, to taste
Pepper, to taste
½ Can Tomato Sauce
1 Med. Onion, sliced
12 Ozs. Sauterne Wine
1 Can Black Olives
½ C. Raisins

Cut the chicken into serving pieces, dust well in flour. Sauté in olive oil in a large roaster or Dutch oven, until browned. Add the Worcestershire sauce, salt, pepper, tomato sauce, onion, and Sauterne wine. Bring to a light boil, lower heat to a simmer, cover and cook 2 hours. During the last 30 minutes, add the olives and raisins.

FIRST NATIVE SON OF CALIFORNIA

Mariano G. Vallejo eventually came to own most of the fertile land in Sonoma Valley and a tract from the Carquinez Straits to Petaluma- together totalling about 248,262 acres or 400 square miles. This rancho had 50,000 cattle, 24,000 sheep, and 8,000 horses. Vallejo, a valiant Californio and amigo de los Americanos, helped with the framing of the state's first American Constitution. The M.G. Vallejo Winery in Glen Ellen celebrates the Californio heritage with its prize winning Chardonnays.

STUFFING FOR CHICKEN, DUCK OR FOWL

Livers
Gizzards
Beef, fat removed
1 T. Flour
1 Sm. Onion, chopped
2-3 Green Chiles, roasted, peeled, chopped
1 Med. Tomato, chopped
Butter for sautéing
2 Oz. Wine Vinegar
½ Tsp. Sugar
12 Black or Green Olives, pits removed
½ C. Raisins
1 Pinch of Nutmeg (optional)
2 Eggs, hard boiled, chopped up

Take the livers, gizzards, and a piece of lean beef of the same size and boil them. Brown the flour in a non-stick sauté pan. Set it aside. When the meats are cool enough to work with, chop them fine. Sauté the onion, green chiles, and tomato in butter. Add the chopped meats. Heat through to mix. Add 2 Ozs. vinegar mixed with 2 Oz. water. Add ½ Tsp. sugar and the browned flour, olives, raisins, the optional nutmeg, and 2 hard boiled eggs. Stir up together, and cover until the mass obtains consistency, when it is ready for use.

Gallina con Garbanzos

FRIED CHICKEN AND PEAS

1 T. Olive Oil
Chicken giblets
1 Med. Onion, sliced
½ Tsp. Parsley, minced
1 Lemon Peel, grated
1 Chicken fryer, cut up in pieces for frying
Several slices of Bacon or Ham (only for flavoring)
Salt
2 Green Chiles, roasted, peeled, chopped
1 Tsp. Olive Oil
1 Tsp. California Salad Vinegar (see recipe)
2 T. Parsley, minced
1 Qt. Green Peas, fresh

Heat the olive oil in a large sauté pan. When hot, add the giblets, ½ of the sliced onion, parsley, and the grated lemon peel. Fry slowly to prevent the parsley from turning brown. Put the ham or bacon and the chicken pieces into the frying giblets. Increase the heat a little. Sauté the meats until brown, about 20 to 25 minutes. Remove the ham or bacon.

In a separate pot, put in a little of the chicken's cooking juices, strained. Next add salt, the chiles, olive oil, and vinegar. Add the browned meats, the remainder of the sliced onions, and 2 T. Parsley, minced. Last, put in the green peas and cook, covered, until the peas are done, about 10 to 15 minutes. Serve with the peas in the center and the chicken piled about.

Guajolote en Mole
TURKEY IN PEANUT SAUCE

1 Turkey, cut up
1 Lb. Red Chiles, dry
1 Lb. Chile Ancho
1 Lb. Chile Pasilla
1 C. Peanuts, raw, skinned
1 C. Almonds, whole, skinned
1 C. Walnut pieces
1 Cinnamon stick (2-3 inches long)
Pinch Cumin Seed
Mexican Chocolate (2 pieces)
1 Piece of lean Pork
2 T. Sesame seeds

Boil the turkey pieces until tender and save the broth. Remove all the seeds and veins from the chiles. Throw away the veins, but toast the seeds with the peanuts, almonds, walnuts, cinnamon, cumin seed and the chocolate on a slow flame, stirring constantly. The first change in color or the aroma rising indicates when they are done. Remove and set aside.

Fry the chiles until brown, remove and grind to a smooth paste with some of the reserved broth. Fry all the paste a second time to heat through, then mix with the turkey broth. Put the turkey meat in a deep pan with a small piece of lean pork, pour the mole sauce over and bake at 350 degrees for 1 hour. While the turkey is baking, toast the sesame seeds. Set them aside. Serve with a sprinkling of toasted sesame seeds on top.

Variation: Use a chicken instead of a turkey. Use pine nuts in place of almonds.

CHICKEN PACHECO

Meat from one Chicken, skin removed, diced
8 Ozs. Mushrooms, in a jar, cut into quarters. Reserve liquid.
2 T. Butter
2 T. Flour
1 Tsp. Salt
¼ Tsp. Black Pepper
¼ Tsp. Celery Salt
Pinch of Mace
Milk
Crackers, made into crumbs
Bits of Butter

Mix the meat from the chicken and add the mushrooms. Make a roux of 2 T. butter and 2 T. flour. When brown and smooth, add the salt, pepper, celery salt, and mace. Add the reserved liquor from the mushrooms, mixing it with enough milk to make 2 C. and heat through. Put the meat into a baking dish, pour the sauce over, cover with cracker crumbs, dotting with bits of butter. Bake in 350 degree oven for 50 minutes.

❖

INNOCENT DAYS WITH CONCRETE TO COME

As late as 1887, Los Angeles still had no paved streets, although a paved sidewalk existed around the Temple Block, now the Courthouse Area. After a succession of rains, Angeleños came downtown to work one morning to find all the streets covered with little mounds of earth resembling graves. Into each little mound imitation tombstones were inserted bearing inscriptions such as the following: "Beware of Quicksand! Fare for Ferrying Across, 25 Cents. No Duck-Hunting Allowed In This Pond! Boats Leave This Landing Every Half-Hour."

❖

Espalette
CHICKEN CONTRA COSTA

2 Lg. Tomatoes, chopped
2 Green Chiles, roasted, peeled, chopped
1 Sm. Onion, chopped
1 Clove Garlic, chopped
1 T. Butter
1 T. Water
2 T. Cornmeal
½ Tsp. Salt
1 Chicken, cooked, skin removed, and shredded
Paprika
Butter

Dressing:
2 Egg Yolks, hardboiled
1 Tsp. Butter
½ C. Olive Oil
Sugar to taste
Salt to taste
Juice of ½ Lemon
½ C. Milk, boiling

For Garnish:
Olives
Cheese Fingers

Take the tomatoes, chiles, onion, and garlic and boil covered in the butter and water until they are soft, about 10 minutes. Then add the cornmeal and salt, mixing to make a paste-like consistency. Take the shredded chicken and dust with paprika. Butter a baking dish and pour and spread a layer of the tomato paste mix, using approximately ½ the paste. Next place the chicken pieces. Add the remaining paste over the chicken. Bake in a 375 degree oven for 40 minutes.

To make the dressing, take the yolks of 2 hardboiled eggs and beat them into a powder. Add the butter, olive oil, sugar, salt, and juice of the lemon. Beat well together. Add the boiling milk, stirring.

To serve, pour the dressing over the chicken. Garnish with olives and cheese fingers.

Variation: Use tongue instead of chicken.

Croqueta California
CALIFORNIA CROQUETTES

From *The Times Prize Cook-Book, 453 Good Recipes by California House-Keepers,* comes a recipe from a Mrs. M. S. T. Chisholm of Pico Heights. Whether she was of the Chisholm Trail fame is unknown. One thing is certain, however, her recipe is definitely on the Gourmet Trail. She says: "I have had great success with this in Ensenada." The recipe calls for a mixture of chicken meat, gizzards, and livers to make the two cups.

2 Eggs, well beaten
2 C. Chicken, gizzard and livers, cooked and chopped fine
1 T. Cilantro, chopped
Truffles or Mushrooms, minced, to taste
1 Red Chile, minced
1 Green Chile, minced
¼ C. Gorgonzola cheese, chopped fine
Chicken stock, to moisten
Cracker crumbs
Oil for deep frying

Mix all of the ingredients together except the cracker crumbs and oil. Roll into balls. Roll in cracker crumbs and deep fry.

Roasting the Chiles at the E.C. Ortega Company
Security Pacific Historical Photograph Collection, Los Angeles Public Library

CHAPTER 9

Vegetables
&
Chiles Rellenos

Calabasas Calabasas
CALABASAS CALABASH

    4 Summer Squash
    1 Egg, beaten
    ¼ C. Bread crumbs
    Grated Cheese
    Salt
    Chile Powder
    Butter
    Red Serranos or Jalapeños, cut in strips
    Cilantro
    Butter

Cook the summer squash in salted water until tender, about 15 minutes. Let cool slightly, slice lengthwise, and remove centers. Mix the chopped centers with the egg, bread crumbs, grated cheese, salt, and chile powder. Refill the center of the squash, pile high, sprinkle with more cheese and bits of butter. Bake in a 450 degree oven, 15 to 20 minutes. Garnish with bits of red chile strips and chopped cilantro mixed with a little hot butter.

Esparragos á la Amecameca
AMECAMECA ASPARAGUS

    2 Lbs. Asparagus, freshly peeled
    ½ Lb. Monterey Jack or Yellow Longhorn Cheese, grated
    ½ C. Cream
    8 Black Olives, chopped
    Parsley
    2 T. Chile Sauce No. 1 or more to taste
    2 T. Tomato Sauce or more to taste
    Breadcrumbs

Clean and peel the skin of the asparagus. Layer a glass casserole with them, the cheese, cream, olives, and parsley. Make a second layer the same as the first. Cover the top layer with the chile sauce, tomato sauce, and bread-crumbs and bake in a pre-heated 400 degree oven for 15 minutes.

Spinaca a la Jardin
GARDEN SPINACH

    6 Bunches Spinach, cleaned and stemmed
    1 Clove Garlic, peeled
    Water
    Salt
    1 T. Flour, heaping
    8 Oz. Butter
    8 Oz. Cream
    8 Oz. Canned Mushrooms slices or bits
    2 Eggs, hardboiled and sliced

Wash the spinach thoroughly. Put a clove of garlic in enough boiling water to hold the spinach, add the spinach and simmer 10 minutes. Thoroughly drain the spinach and process until a purée. Set aside momentarily.

Brown the flour in the melted butter. Add the cream and mushrooms stir to mix. Add the spinach purée and bring to a simmer for 10 minutes. When ready to serve, top with sliced hardboiled eggs.

Papas a la Reina
THE QUEEN'S POTATOES

    6 Lg. boiling Potatoes
    Water
    Salt
    ½ Lb. Butter, room temperature
    ½ C. Sugar
    ¼ Lb. Citron peel, chopped
    4 Eggs, well beaten
    ¼ C. Currants
    2 T. Baking Powder

Boil the potatoes with salt and peel them when they are done. Mash them thoroughly and add the remaining ingredients. Place the mix in a greased baking pan and bake for 20 minutes in a 400 degree oven. The baking powder will keep the potatoes fluffy even when re-heated the next day.

Ejotes Californio
EARLY CALIFORNIA SNAP BEANS

The original recipe called for *cooking compound*, for which Maggi Seasoning has been substituted. Use a bouillion cube if no Maggi Seasoning is available. If you use plain water, add 1 T. salt to it. Omit the sugar, if necessary, but it is a very small amount, only there to brighten the flavor of the tomatoes.

2 Lbs. Green Beans
2 Dashes Maggi Seasoning
1 Med. Onion, chopped
2 Green Chiles, roasted, peeled, seeded and chopped
1 C. Tomatoes, fresh or canned
½ Tsp. Sugar
Salt
2 T. Flour
1 Qt. Water, hot

Cut the beans in 1 inch lengths. To a sauté pan add the Maggi Seasoning, beans, onion, chiles, tomatoes, sugar, and salt. Sauté for 5 minutes. Add the flour to coat the ingredients. Add the hot water and simmer 45 minutes.

Variations: Use 1 lb. beans, 1 C. green tomatoes, a pinch of baking soda, and 3 cloves garlic. Use 3 cups water instead of a quart. Omit the green chiles and Maggi Seasoning. Brown the garlic in 2 T. bacon fat, remove it, brown the onions. Add the tomatoes, sautéing them lightly, add the beans, water, and baking soda. Partially cover and simmer until liquid is completely reduced and beans are tender. Season with salt and vinegar.

Elotes de Los Angeles
CORN A LA GRATIN

1 Tsp. Butter
1 Can Corn
1 Can Green Chiles, chopped
½ C. Monterey Jack Cheese, grated
⅓ C. Raisins

Heat the butter in a sauté pan, add the corn and chiles, and sauté 5 minutes. Add the cheese and lastly the raisins. Place in a baking dish in a 400 degree oven until the cheese is well melted. Serve with bread and butter.
Variation: Use 4 ounces grated Parmesan cheese.

Macarrón Mexicano
Mexican Macaroni

For the Sauce:
1 Onion, chopped
1 Bunch Parsley, chopped,
1 Bunch Celery, finely chopped
Olive oil
8 Oz. can Tomato Sauce

For the Pasta:
1 Lb. Macaroni
Salted Water
Pineapple Cream Cheese (Kraft makes this)
1-2 Hardboiled Eggs, chopped

In a deep pan, sauté the onion, parsley and celery in olive oil until a light brown. Add the tomato sauce and simmer for 15 minutes.
In boiling, salted water, cook the pasta *al dente*. When done, drain and rinse and keep hot. In a oven casserole put a layer of macaroni, and a layer of sauce, then sprinkle with tiny bits of the pineapple cream cheese. If necessary, put in a 400 degree oven for 10 minutes, or until cheese is runny. Top with the hardboiled eggs.

PRICKLY PEAR

If fresh *nopales* are purchased, they must have their *agujas* or spines removed before cooking. To do this, wear rubber gloves. Using a vegetable peeler, scrape off each spine, low enough to insure its removal. Scrape off around the edge of each *nopal* and cut off the 1 inch to 1½ inch of the woody stem end. Some larger markets catering to the Mexican community have fresh, cleaned, and chopped *nopalitos* ready to cook.

1 Lb. *Nopales*
2 Slices Bacon
2 Tomatoes, chopped
1 Med. Onion, chopped
1 New Mexican Green Chile, roasted, peeled, and chopped
1 Clove of Garlic, or to taste, chopped
1 Tsp. Salt
¼ Tsp. Pepper

Chop the *nopales* into *nopalitos*. That is, into a large dice. Some prefer them cut into string bean size morsels. Into enough boiling water to well cover, put the chopped or sliced nopalitos. Boil with a penny or other copper coin in the pot about 8 minutes. The coin prevents the ooze of the nopales from boiling over.

Sauté the bacon in a skillet, remove when done and drain the strips on toweling. Sauté the tomatoes, onion, green chile, and garlic in the bacon fat for about 5 minutes. When lightly browned, add salt and pepper. Taste for seasonings. Drain the *nopalitos* thoroughly, add to the sautéed ingredients, toss and re-heat through, about 5 to 10 minutes on low heat. Crumble the bacon and add to the mixture before serving.

Colache
SUMMER SQUASH SUCCOTASH

This was originally an Indian dish, but the Californios refined it somewhat.

2 Lbs. Summer Squash
1 Lb. String Beans, diced
1 Med. Onion, chopped
2 Green Chiles, roasted, peeled, chopped
2 Lg. Tomatoes, chopped
1 Clove of Garlic, minced
2 T. Olive Oil
½ Tsp. Pepper
1 T. Wine Vinegar
1 Tsp. Salt
½ C. Water, boiling (if necessary)
3 Ears Fresh Corn, kernels cut from the cob

Wash and dice the squash and green beans. Add the onion, chile, tomatoes, garlic, and seasoning. Heat the oil in a stock pot and add the vegetables and remaining ingredients (except the water) and saute slowly. Add ½ C. boiling water if necessary. When the beans are tender, add the corn cut from the cob. Cook another 10 to 15 minutes, or until corn is cooked.

A DRAMATIC DROP IN THE COST OF TRAVEL

In 1860, a trip via wagon between St. Louis and Los Angeles cost $200.00. In March of 1886, railroad fares between Kansas City and Los Angeles dropped from $10 to $5 and finally to $1 during a fare war between the AT&SF and the Southern Pacific. People from all over the country rushed to purchase tickets. The fare war lasted approximately a year and gave rise to the local wisdom that a native was anyone who had resided in town longer than twenty-four hours.

Quelites San Vicente
SOLDIERS' GREENS

2 C. Water
2 Lbs. Spinach or Mustard Greens
2 Scallions
1 Clove of Garlic, minced
½ Tsp. Salt
1 Strip Bacon
2 T. Olive Oil (optional)

Put the water on to boil. Clean and stem the spinach or mustard greens. Mince the scallions and garlic, set aside momentarily. Steam the greens over the 2 cups of water, about 5 minutes. Remove, cool and chop them finely, seasoning with salt. In a large skillet, cook the bacon strip, when crisp, remove and wrap in a paper towel. Reserve the bacon fat, keeping a low flame under it. Next, wilt the scallions and garlic in the bacon fat or olive oil in a skillet large enough to hold the greens. Add the chopped greens to the skillet and simmer for 5 minutes. Crumble the bacon and sprinkle it over the greens. Toss well and serve with meat dishes.

Calabacitas con Chile Verde
SONORATOWN SUCCULENT SQUASH

2 Med. Onions, chopped
½ Lb. Salt Pork, chopped
2 Summer Squash, sliced
15 Oz. can of Corn or 6 ears, fresh, kernels removed
6 Green Chiles, roasted, peeled, chopped
1-2 Oz. Cream, at room temperature

Sauté the onions with the salt pork. Then add the vegetables and enough water to cook well. When the water has almost evaporated and the vegetables start to look dry, pour a little cream on top. Heat through without letting the cream boil.

Espárragos de Alhambra

ASPARAGUS ALHAMBRA

2 Bunches Asparagus, peeled and tied into 3 bunches
1 Tsp. Salt for each bunch

For the Sauce:
2 T. Butter
1 Sm. White Onion, diced small
1 Bay Laurel Leaf
6 Peppercorns
3 T. Flour
2 C. Stock (chicken or veal)
Pinch of Nutmeg
2 Eggs
1 T. Lemon Juice
1 T. Butter, scant
Toast

Cover the asparagus with water and boil them for 10 minutes. Add 2 Tsp. salt and simmer 5 minutes longer.

In a sauté pan put the butter, onion, bay leaf, peppercorns, and sauté on a low flame so as not to brown the onion. Next add the flour and stock. Season the sauce with a pinch of nutmeg and simmer all together for about 20 minutes. Strain the sauce and return it to the pan. Put on lowest flame so it will not boil. Beat the eggs very lightly, together with the lemon juice. Gradually add the egg-lemon juice to the sauce, stirring constantly. Next add the scant tablespoon of butter. Serve the asparagus on toast with the sauce in a gravy boat or bowl.

EMBARCADERO ENTRÉE

For the Sauce:
¼ C. Olive Oil
2 T. Butter
2 Scallions, chopped
1 Bunch Parsley, chopped fine
1-2 Stalks of Celery, peeled and finely chopped
1 Leek, cleaned and chopped
1-2 Cloves of Garlic, or to taste
1-2 Green Chiles, roasted, peeled, chopped
Salt
1 T. Chorizo Sausage
½ C. Meat or Vegetable Stock

For the Entrée:
½ Lb. Macaroni
Edam Cheese, grated

Make a sauce of the oil and butter; in this sauté the scallions, parsley, celery, leek, garlic, and green chile. Season with salt and the chorizo sausage, broken into small bits. After the sauce is reduced quite well, add the stock.

Boil the macaroni until *al dente*. Rinse with hot water. Place the pasta on a warmed platter, pour the hot sauce over it and cover the top with grated Edam cheese.

STUFFED POTATOES

1½ Lbs. Potatoes
Milk for mashing
Salt and pepper to taste
Chile powder
Some leftover Roast Beef
¼ C. Golden Raisins
2 Eggs, hardboiled and chopped
¼ C. Black Olives
Pinch of ground Cloves
Port Wine
Oil for frying

Boil and mash the potatoes with milk, season highly with salt, pepper, and mild chile powder. Set aside to cool. Chop the beef and mix with the raisins, eggs, and olives, seasoning with a pinch of cloves. Moisten the mixture with a little port wine and form into cones. Beat the potatoes until they are light and fluffy. Cover the cones with the potatoes and deep-fry in hot oil until they turn a golden brown. Drain on toweling and serve.

❀

SIX TO ONE THE HOUSE BURNS DOWN BEFORE EITHER ONE GETS THERE

Gambling, a popular recreation even with the social elite of Los Angeles, reached a new high with the coming of the Confidence Engine Co. No. 2. It was the second fire brigade in Los Angeles. The first company was known as the 38's Fire Company. These two brigades came into competition to see who could reach the fire first. Many an alarm was sounded to allow the boys in the brigade to stake their bets.

❀

Budin de Verduras
VEGETABLE CASSEROLE

⅔ C. Snap Beans
⅔ C. Carrots
⅔ C. Peas
5 T. Butter
½ Tsp. Baking Soda
1 Pt. boiling Water
3 T. Flour
1 Pt. Milk
Salt and pepper to taste
1 Lemon, for juice
⅓ C. Monterey Jack Cheese
3 Egg yolks, beaten
3 T. Toasted Bread, in bits

Clean and chop the beans into bite-size morsels. Peel and quarter the carrots. Sauté the beans, carrots, and peas in 2 T. butter for a moment and add the baking soda and boiling water. Cover and simmer for 50 minutes. This should become well cooked, but not watery.

To 3 T. melted butter add 3 T. flour, sauté a moment without giving color to the flour and then add the milk. Beat this with a rotary beater and when it begins to boil, remove from the fire, and season with salt, pepper, and lemon juice to taste. Add the cheese and well beaten egg yolks. Mix the sauce well, pour over the vegetables, and place them in a buttered baking dish. Sprinkle with toasted bread bits. Bake in a 350 degree for 50 minutes. Pour out onto a heated serving platter.

Croquetas de Garbanzos
CHICKPEA CROQUETTES

Canned garbanzos work fine here. Heat and mash them in their canned juice.

1 C. Garbanzo Beans, cooked
1 T. Grated Parmesan Cheese
Large pinch of Chile Piquin or Cayenne powder
Salt and pepper to taste
1 Egg, beaten
½ C. Breadcrumbs, toasted
Olive oil
Prepared Spanish Sauce (see recipe)
1 Tomato, sliced
1 Tsp. Parsley, minced

Mash the garbanzos while they are hot. Add the cheese, chile powder, salt and black pepper to taste. Form then into croquettes, dip in the beaten egg, roll in the toasted breadcrumbs and sauté in hot oil. Drain well before serving. Pour the Spanish sauce over the garbanzos and garnish with the tomato and parsley.

Col Rellena
PORK-STUFFED CABBAGE

The sauce is somewhat important to this dish. The tomatoes should be roasted and almost approach a purée, when chopped. But there should still be some chunky bits remaining.

For the Cabbage:
1 Lb. firm Cabbage
Water
1 Tsp. Salt
1 Clove of Garlic, minced
½ Lb. Pork, ground
2 T. Olives, minced
½ Tsp. pickled Chiles Serranos or Jalapeños, minced
½ Tsp. whole Capers
1 Egg, hardboiled chopped
1 T. ground Almonds
1 C. hot Water
Cheesecloth

For the Sauce:
½ Clove of Garlic, minced
1 Tsp. Onion, minced
½ C. cold Water
2 C. fresh Tomatoes, peeled, and finely chopped

Boil the cabbage in salted water with the minced garlic for 15 minutes. Using a large slotted spoon, take the cabbage from the water and drain it. When it is cold enough to touch, but still somewhat warm, remove the heart, being careful not to unfasten the outer leaves.

Mix the remaining cabbage and ingredients together and fill the cabbage. Rearrange the cabbage leaves to once again make it look like a head of cabbage. Enclose the head in a large square of cheesecloth, and tie it closed. Place in a deep stockpot with a cup of hot water, cover and steam for 30 minutes.

Cook all the sauce ingredients together until thick. Pour over the cabbage when it is ready to serve.

Habas Carioca
LIMA BEANS CARIOCA STYLE

Here is a merciful change from buttered lima beans.

1 C. Lima Beans, dry
Salt
2 T. Vegetable Oil
1 T. Onion, minced
1 T. Parsley, minced
Dash of mild Chile Powder
2 T. Green Chiles, roasted, peeled, chopped
1 C. Tomatoes, strained
½ Tsp. Hot Chile Powder

Soak the beans overnight. Discard the water, cover the beans with fresh boiling water and simmer until tender, adding salt when the beans are partially cooked.

In hot oil or bacon fat, sauté the onion, parsley, chiles and mild chile powder for 5 minutes. Add the tomatoes, hot chile powder and cooked beans. Season with salt and pepper. Simmer to allow the beans to absorb some of the cooking stock. Serve hot.

Zanahorias en Mole
CARROTS IN SALSA MOLE

Use the very largest carrots available.

6 Lg. Carrots
½ C. Monterey Jack Cheese, grated
1 Egg, separated
½ Tsp. Flour
Bacon Fat or Olive Oil

For the Sauce:
1 Sm. jar of Mole Sauce
1 C. Water

Peel and boil the carrots; slice lengthwise and carefully remove the carrot heart and fill the cavity with cheese. Beat egg white, add to it a well-beaten egg yolk and the flour. Beat all together thoroughly. In this egg mixture, roll the carrots and fry them in a little bacon fat or olive oil.

Cook the sauce ingredients to a thick purée. Pour the sauce over the carrots and serve.

❀

NOT THE PEPPER IN THESE RECIPES, HOWEVER

There were no shade trees in the entire downtown area of Los Angeles from the 1850s to 1860s until John Temple and Charlie Ducommon planted pepper trees (genus Schinus) in front of their block-long properties. These acts became the gossip of 1861, according to the Star, Los Angeles' first newspaper.

❀

Nopalitos con Camarones
SANTA MONICA SHRIMP AND NOPALES

1 Jar of *Nopales*, about 10 ounces, drained
1 C. Tomatoes, strained
1 Med. Onion, white, minced
1 Clove of Garlic, minced
6 Chiles Serranos, peeled, seeded and minced
¼ Tsp. White Pepper
½ Tsp. Salt
3 Eggs, separated
1 Can of Shrimps, about 6 ounces
2 T. Bacon Fat
2 T. Cilantro or Parsley, finely chopped

Chop the *nopales* into bite size bits. Set them aside. In a saucepot, put the tomatoes, minced onion, garlic, chiles serranos, salt and white pepper. Cook slowly for 5 minutes to form a thick paste. Mix the *nopales* with this sauce. Put it into a 300 degree oven to heat thoroughly.

Beat the whites of the eggs until they are very stiff. Add the well beaten yolks with a little salt. Pass each shrimp through the egg mixture. Sauté quickly in the bacon grease in a skillet, browning the shrimp on both sides. Place each shrimp on the hot *nopal*. Garnish with cilantro and serve.

Variation: Substitute 6 T. dried shrimp for the can above. Rinse them in a cup of water to remove a little of the salty taste, if preferred.

Chayotes Rellenos en Estilo Californio Sur

CITRON STUFFED SQUASH SOUTHERN CALIFORNIA STYLE

6 medium Chayotes
Water
Cinnamon and Sugar to taste
1 C. Melted butter
½ C. Raisins, minced
½ C. candied Citron, minced
½ C. Almonds, minced
Breadcrumbs
Butter for topping
Tomato slices

Cut the chayotes along the length to make halves. Put them into boiling water sufficient to cover. When they are tender, take out the pulp, but do not break the skin. Mash the pulp with sugar, cinnamon, and melted butter. Add the minced raisins, citron, and almonds and mix well. Refill the shells, cover with breadcrumbs, dot with butter and bake in a 350 degree oven until browned on top. Serve on a heated platter garnished with tomato slices.

Quingombó Quema

OAKLAND OKRA

4 C. Okra, fresh and tender
½ C. Olive Oil or Butter
1 Lg. White Onion, chopped
2 C. Tomato Purée
2 Chiles Jalapeños, seeded and minced
Cayenne powder to taste
1 T. Parsley, minced
1½ Tsp. Oregano, fresh or ½ tsp. dried
Salt and pepper
1 C. Monterey Jack Cheese, grated

Wash, drain, dry, and slice the okra into rounds about ½ inch long. Heat the oil or butter while slicing the okra. Sauté the okra in a cast iron skillet until it does not stick. Add the onion and continue to sauté a few minutes. Next, add the tomato purée, jalapeños, cayenne parsley, oregano, salt and pepper, and continue to simmer until the okra is tender. Add the grated cheese and stir.

Variation: Blanch the okra in boiling water for about 2 minutes before sauteeing.

Papas en Mole Poblano
POTATOES IN MOLE POBLANO

1 Jar Mole Poblano
2 C. Beef Stock
½ C. Olive Oil
6 Med. Boiled Potatoes
1 T. Cilantro, minced

Dissolve the mole in 1 C. of the stock. Heat the oil and slowly simmer the dissolved mole in it for 10 minutes. Add the remaining stock. Peel and slice the potatoes and add them to the simmering pot. Let simmer another 5 minutes, pour all into a buttered casserole, sprinkle with cilantro and serve while hot.

Cebollitas Criollas
CREOLE STYLE ONIONS

The rage for Cajun food was not new in the 1980s. This recipe, adapted from *Ramona's Spanish-Mexican Cookery*, published in 1929, is a quick, savory dish!

4 Slices of Bacon
4 C. Scallions, minced
Salt and pepper to taste
2 T. Wine Vinegar
2 Eggs, hardboiled
Pinch Chile Piquin or Cayenne powder

Dice the bacon and sauté until brown, add the minced scallions, salt and pepper. Sauté 5 minutes, add the vinegar and cover to simmer until done, 5 minutes longer. Serve, covering the top with minced hardboiled eggs sprinkled with chile powder.

Chile Maron y Calabasas con Arroz
BULL NOSE CHILES, SQUASH AND RICE

½ C. Olive Oil
1½ C. Rice
2 Cloves of Garlic, minced
½ C. minced Scallions, green parts included
1 C. Tomato Sauce
1 C. Meat or Vegetable Stock
1 Tsp. Serrano or Jalapeño chiles, minced
1 C. rounded Green Bell Pepper, chopped
1 C. rounded Green Squash, chopped
1 Tsp. sweet Paprika
1 Tsp. Oregano
Salt to taste
1 T. Cilantro, minced
Chile sauce from Chapter 2
Sliced Avocados

Heat the olive oil in a large skillet and sauté the rice until it colors a little. Add the garlic and scallions and stir constantly, about 2 minutes. Next, add the tomato sauce, and enough stock to cover well the mixture. Lastly, add the chiles, bell pepper, squash, paprika, oregano, and salt. Stir well for the last time, cover and simmer slowly, or put the dish in the oven at 300 degrees and bake until near dry. Garnish with the cilantro. Serve with chile sauce of choice and sliced avocados.

A LANDMARK IN THE HISTORY OF CHILE

Émile Ortega, native Santa Barbaran, was for a while, sheriff of Ventura County, where much of his land holdings were. By the late 1800s, there were few bandidos *remaining to be tracked down, so Ortega opened the first chile cannery on the West Coast. His secret was in fire roasting the chiles to remove their skins. In 1898, he opened a packing house in Ventura, California, but due to increased demand, he moved the plant to Los Angeles several years later.*

CALIFORNIA STUFFED CHILES

A prepared sauce from Chapter 2 may be served over the chiles, or a white sauce with apples, raisins, peach preserves, or marmalade added to desired taste.

The Chiles:
1 C. Beef, Veal or Chicken
1 T. Onion, chopped fine
1 Clove of Garlic, minced
½ C. Tomatoes, chopped fine
½ C. Olives, sliced
¼ C. Raisins, chopped
1 T. Vinegar
2 T. Olive Oil or Bacon fat
8 Green Chiles, roasted, peeled and seeded

The Dipping Batter:
2 Eggs
2 Tsp. Flour
2 Tsp. Milk
Salt to taste
Red Chile Powder to taste
Olive Oil for frying
Chopped cilantro for garnish

Combine the first six ingredients. Add 1 T. mild vinegar and cook all in 2 T. olive oil. Allow to cool and then stuff the chiles.

Beat the eggs and add the flour and milk. Stir to the consistency of a sticky batter. Season the batter with salt and red pepper, to taste. Dip the chiles in the batter, and fry golden-brown in hot olive oil. Drain, sprinkle with chopped cilantro and serve hot.

Chiles Maron Rellenos
CALIFORNIA STUFFED BULL NOSE CHILES

1 Cup Beef or Pork, ground
½ C. Bread, chopped
2 T. Onion
½ C. Tomatoes
1 T. Sugar
½ C. Raisins
1 T. Butter
1 Egg, beaten
Salt to taste
Chile Powder to taste
2 Green or Red Bell Peppers
1 C. Tomatoes, chopped
Salt
Oregano
Bread Crumbs

Mix 1 C. ground meat, any kind, with ½ C. chopped bread. Set aside.

Cook the onion, tomatoes, sugar, and raisins together in the butter for a few minutes. Let cool. Add the egg, salt, and chile powder. Add the ground meat mixture and mix well.

Cut the bell peppers in half, seed and devein. Then fill them with the stuffing. Set the halves close together in an au gratin pan and fill in between with raw tomato, salt, and a pinch of oregano. Fill enough to reach near the top edge of the pan. Sprinkle with bread crumbs and bake until well done and brown, in a moderate oven.

Chiles Maron con Sardinas
BELL PEPPERS WITH SARDINES

4 Bell Peppers
½ C. Vinegar
½ C. Water
1 Clove Garlic
½ Tsp. Oregano
3 Inch piece of Cinnamon
1 Tin Sardines, packed in oil, boned and skinned
Lemon juice
½ C. Bread
1 T. Onion, chopped
½ C. Tomato, chopped
1 T. Olives, sliced
6 Raisins
Butter
Bread crumbs, for filling
Grated cheese, for filling

Roast, peel, seed, and devein the green bell peppers. Mix the peppers with a ½ C. vinegar, ½ C. water simmered with ½ garlic clove, oregano, cinnamon, and soak them all night. Soak the sardines in a little lemon juice or vinegar to clean them of their packing oil. Mash them well. Make a filling of the sardines, bread, onion, tomatoes, sliced olives, and raisins. Drain the peppers and fill them with the filling. Cover with melted butter, bread crumbs and grated cheese. Bake in 350 degree oven for 20 minutes, with 2 T. water in the bottom of the pan or casserole dish. Serve hot.

Variation: Mash the sardines and finely grated cheese with the other stuffing ingredients, then proceed.

Fritada de Queso y Chile
CALIFORNIA CHEESE AND CHILE FRITTERS

8 Pasilla or fresh Green Chiles
1 Lb. of Monterrey Jack, grated
2 pieces Bread
½ C. Tomato juice
Salt
Pinch of Chile Piquin or Cayenne powder
2 Eggs, beaten
Bread Crumbs
Olive Oil for frying
2 C. Prepared Spanish Sauce (see recipe)
4 Eggs, hardboiled and sliced

Roast the green chiles and seed and devein them. Fill each with a mixture of grated cheese, bread soaked in tomato juice, salt and crumbled Piquin. Fasten with toothpicks and dip in whipped egg. Next roll them in bread crumbs. Fry in olive oil. Serve with Prepared Sauce and a circle of sliced hard-boiled eggs.

ETHNIC FOOD DIVERSITY

Chun Chick, a former resident of San Francisco, opened the first Chinese market in Los Angeles in 1861–a combination curiosity shop and grocery store. Also, the influx of Chinese brought about many vegetable truck farms. These "trucks" would be wheeled by the residences, and the truckers would shout out the names of their produce. At one point in time, they all went on strike as prices had fallen precipitously.

Cebollas Rellenos al Horno
STUFFED AND BAKED SPANISH ONIONS

6 Med. Onions
12 Oz. of cooked Bacon or Chorizo
6 Oz. Breadcrumbs
¼ Tsp. Mace, ground
Salt and Pepper to taste
5 T. Cream
6 T. Butter
1 T. Flour
½ Lemon

From the six onions, slice ⅛ to ¼ inch off the top. Scoop out the centers and chop them. Parboil the onion shells in water for 3 minutes, then drain them upside down. Mix the minced bacon or chorizo with the minced onion hearts. Add the breadcrumbs, mace, salt, pepper, and 1 T. cream. Stuff the mixture into well-drained onion shells.

In a large metal baking dish, put the 6 T. butter, warming the dish in the oven enough to melt the butter. Remove and put the onions in the baking dish. When done, carefully put the onions on a serving platter. Put the dish into the 350 degree oven for 1 hour basting frequently. Brown 1 T. flour and set aside. Add the juice of the ½ lemon, 4 T. cream and a little browned flour to the sauce. Bring to a boil and pour over the baked onions.

Cebollas con Picadillo de Escabeche

SPANISH ONIONS WITH SAUCY STUFFING

2 Large White Onions
2 T. Flour
2 T. Butter
2 T. Onion, chopped
2 T. Olives, sliced
2 T. Raisins
2 T. Dill Pickle, chopped
1 T. Cilantro
2 T. Nuts, chopped
½ C. Bread crumbs
½ C. Chicken shredded, cooked
Salt to taste
Cheese for melting

Sauce:
1 T. Butter
1 T. Flour
2 T. Lemon juice
½ C. Water
¼ C. Cilantro, finely chopped

Trim the stem and root ends of the onions clean, but don't cut into the onions' flesh. Boil the onions until soft and cut the stem side ½ inch off. Put the tops aside for another use. When cool, remove centers of the onions, chop, and set aside. Brown 2 T. flour in 2 T. butter, to make a roux. Add the chopped onion removed from centers. Next add the sliced olives, raisins, chopped dill pickle, cilantro, chopped nuts, bread crumbs, chicken, and salt. Fill the onions and pile high with the filling. Put a large lump of cheese on top of each and bake in moderate oven 45 minutes. Serve with a sauce made butter and flour, browned together. When browned, add the lemon juice, water, and cilantro.

Papas Rellenos con Tocina y Chiles
STUFFED POTATOES WITH BACON AND CHILES

2 Large Baking Potatoes
Butter or Olive Oil
2 T. Butter
1 T. Cilantro, minced
2 T. Pimiento, chopped
2 T. Cucumber, peeled and seeded
¼ Tsp. Chile Powder
2 T. Milk, hot
½ Egg, whipped
4 Strips of bacon
Cilantro & Pimento garnish

Scrub the potatoes lightly, allow to dry thoroughly. Rub butter or best olive oil on the potatoes. Bake them until soft in a 400 degree oven for 45 minutes. Cut off a slice at one end and cut out the center of the potatoes. Mash the potato centers and add butter, cilantro, pimiento, cucumber, chile powder, hot milk, whipped egg; beat until light, fill the potato shells. Place two strips of bacon on top and bake the potatoes in the oven until the bacon is crisp. Garnish with a stripe of pimiento and chopped cilantro.

Variation: In place of the pimento, use a roasted, marinated red bell pepper.

Fideo al Horno
CALIFORNIO BAKED PASTA

2 C. Macaroni or Spaghetti
¼ C. Olive Oil
1 Clove of Garlic, minced
½ C. Beef Jerky
1 T. Flour
½ C. Mushrooms, chopped
2 T. Green Chile Pulp
1 roasted, marinated Red Bell Pepper, chopped fine
2 C. Tomatoes
Salt, to taste
Queso Mexicano or Monterey Jack cheese, grated

Cook and drain two cups of pasta. Heat the olive oil, add the garlic and jerky, and cook until the beef curls. Add the flour, sauté until brown. Add the chopped mushrooms, green chile pulp, and bell pepper. Lastly, add two cups of tomatoes, cook all together, salt to taste, and mix with the pasta. Put the mixture into a baking dish, cover with *Queso Mexicano*, and bake till the cheese is melted and bubbly hot.

Chiles de Pobladores
PIONEER CHILES

6 Green Chiles
6 strips Cream Cheese, ¼ inch x 5 inches
Flour seasoned with Chile Powder
Salt
2 Eggs, White and Yolks separated
Olive Oil

Roast and peel the chiles. Remove the seed and veins from the chiles; stuff the cream cheese inside. Close them with a toothpick. Add a little flour and a pinch of salt to the whites and beat stiff. Beat the yolks gently until mixed. Fold the yolks into the whites. Dip the chiles in seasoned flour and then into the egg wash. Fry the chiles in hot oil until golden brown. Drain them on paper towels. If liked, cover with Chile Sauce No. 1.
Variation: Add ½ C. raisins. Soak the raisins in some wine if desired.

Chiles Rancheros
RANCH STYLE STUFFED CHILES

From *How We Cook in Los Angeles* comes Mrs. J.G. Downey's recipe for Stuffed Peppers, definitely a hand me down from days of the *ranchos*. John Downey served as Governor of California and the City of Downey, near Los Angeles, is named after him.

12 Lg. Green Chiles
1 Onion, chopped
1 Clove Garlic, minced
½ C. Corn, grated
1 T. Butter
1 C. Tomatoes, chopped
Salt and pepper to taste
1 C. Meat, beef or chicken, minced, pre-cooked
1 Slice of Ham or Bacon
Olive Oil

Sauce:
1 T. Butter
1 T. Flour
1 Onions, minced
1 Tomato, chopped fine
1 Green Chile, chopped fine
2 Sm. Apples, peeled, cored and chopped
Raisins
Olives

Roast, peel, and seed the chiles. Sauté the onion, garlic, and corn in the butter. Add the tomatoes, season with salt and pepper. Reduce heat and allow to simmer slowly for 15 minutes. Add the meat and a small slice of ham to improve the flavor. Heat through. Stuff the chiles, dip in beaten egg, roll in flour. Fry in oil.

Sauté the butter and flour until browned. Add the onions, tomato, chiles, and apples and enough water if necessary, to make a sauce. Cook until reduce to a saucelike consistency. Add the raisins and olives to taste. Put the chiles in this sauce and simmer a moment.

Camarones en Chile
SHRIMP IN CHILES

Sauce:
1 Sm. Onion, minced
2 Med. Tomatoes, chopped fine
1 Green Chile, chopped fine
Garlic (optional)

Chiles:
4 Green Chiles
6-8 Oz. Bay Shrimp, peeled but uncooked
Water
1 Slice Bacon
1 Sm. Onion, chopped
1 Clove Garlic, minced
1 Med. Tomato, chopped
1 T. Parsley, chopped fine
Olive Oil
1 Tsp. Wine Vinegar, or to taste
1 Chile Serrano or other hot chile, chopped
1-2 Cloves, ground
Cinnamon, ground
1 Tsp. Sugar or to taste
Raisins, soaked in wine
Pine nuts, chopped
Almonds, chopped
Capers
1 Egg, hard boiled, chopped fine
Flour for dusting
2 Eggs, beaten for dipping

Garnish:
Cooked Onions
Parsley
Slivered Almonds

Sauté the onion, tomato, chile and optional garlic until the tomato cooks down a bit.

Roast, peel, and seed the chiles. Add the shrimp to 4 C. boiling water to which 1 slice of bacon has been added. Boil 5 minutes. Remove and reserve the cooking liquid. Sauté the onions, garlic, tomato, and parsley in olive oil. Add the shrimp, lower the heat. Add a little vinegar and 1 or 2 T. of the cooking liquid and the hot chiles, cloves, cinnamon, and sugar to taste. Next add in the raisins, pine nuts, almonds, and capers and the chopped hard boiled egg. Fill the chiles with the mixture and close with toothpicks. Dip in egg, roll in seasoned flour. Saute in the the tomato sauce. Garnish with cooked onions, parsley, and slivered almonds.

Rellenos Ternera
VEAL STUFFED CHILES

6 Bell Peppers
1 Lb. Veal, ground
4 Oz. Chorizo Sausage
½ C. Raisins, soaked in wine and drained
½ C. Almonds
3 Eggs, for batter
Flour seasoned with Oregano and Chile Powder
Olive Oil for frying

Prepare the bell peppers by roasting, peeling, and removing the seeds, being careful to keep the size and shape of them as much as possible. To the ground veal add the chorizo, soaked and drained raisins, and coarsely chopped almonds. Moisten this with some veal stock and season with salt. Stuff the chiles, dip in a thin egg batter and seasoned flour and fry in olive oil. Serve with the Prepared Spanish Sauce.

Metate y Mano *grinding the corn for tortillas*
Security Pacific Historical Photograph Collection, Los Angeles Public Library

CHAPTER 10

Tamales & Enchiladas

Beginning Instructions:

When using fresh corn husks for making tamales, cut off about 1 inch of the more pointed end. Rinse under water, simmer 10 minutes and drain and dry the husks before using. Use thin strips of husk to make strings for tying the tamales up.

In all the recipes below, the use of garlic is optional, although recommended. Proportions are only approximate as tastes for garlic vary. The Sweet Tamale recipes, using mostly fruit, are not made with garlic.

The pioneer families were fond of herbs and spices growing wild or cultivated near the kitchen. Copy their imaginative recipes by adding: To chicken tamales, spices such as oregano, cilantro, and bay leaves; to pork tamales, a little prepared mustard; to beef tamales, nutmeg and cloves.

Pastel de Tamal
TAMALE PIE

2 C. Hot Water
½ C. Lard
1 Tsp. Salt
Masa
2 C. cooked Beef, Pork, Veal, or Chicken
Suet
2 T. Masa
½ C. Red Chile Pulp
½ C. Stock or water
Salt to taste
Chile powder

Combine the hot water, melted lard, salt, and enough masa to make thick dough. Spread the dough on the bottom and sides of a pie tin. For a filling mix any 2 cups of the following: beef, pork, veal or chicken with plenty of suet for shortening. Measure 2 C. meat, add the masa, chile pulp, and the meat stock or water. Cook for a few minutes, fill the pie crust, spread more dough over top. Make little balls of masa the size of marbles and set them around the edge. Pour a little melted lard over the top, sprinkle with chile powder. Bake about 30 minutes in a medium oven.

Tamales

1 Lb. Beef, pork, ham or chicken
1 T. Suet or lard (no substitutions)
1 Tsp. Salt
2 Cloves Garlic, peeled and mashed
Warm Water
½ C. Red Chile Pulp
32 Oz. Masa
2 T. Salt
2 T. Lard
Boiling Water
1 Bag of Corn Husks for Tamales

Chop or shred 1 pound of beef, pork, or chicken. Add the suet or lard, salt, and garlic. Fry the mixture in a pan until tender. Chop again very fine and return the mixture to the pan. Add a little warm water and the red chile pulp. Stir and fry few minutes.

To make the masa dough: add to 32 ounces of cornmeal: 2 T. salt, 2 T. lard, and boiling water to make a thick dough. Cut off about 1 inch of corn husk stalk ends and soak in hot water 10 minutes; dry and rub over with hot lard. Put a layer of dough on the husk about 4 inches long, 1 ½ inches wide and ¼ inch thick. Along the center spread 2 Tsp. of the prepared meat. Roll and fold the small end of the husk. Tie the tamales with husk strings and place them folded end down in a strainer over hot water. Cover and steam 3 or 4 hours. Serve hot.

Variations: Sweet Tamales. Omit the meat and salt. Use some of pineapple juice and water to make the masa into a dough. Substitute 2½ T. sugar for all the salt. Use pineapple bits, raisins, almonds, and a pinch or two of ground anise seeds in place of the meat. Mix the sweet with some ground Chile powder or pulp and follow all the other instructions. Make a purée of strawberries. Use the purée to form the masa dough. Add raisins soaked overnight in claret or sherry. Serve as a dessert tamale. The strawberry purée will color the dough a beautiful color.

Tamales de Pollo
CHICKEN TAMALES

1 Bag of Corn Husks
Lard
1 Chicken
32 Oz. Masa
Water
4 cloves Garlic, minced
Salt to taste
½ Tsp. Anise Seeds, ground
1 T. Red Chile Pulp or 1 T. Chile Powder
1 T. Lard
1 Tsp. Marjoram or Oregano
Chile Sauce No. 1 for mixing
¼ C. Olives, chopped
¼ C. Raisins, whole or chopped
Salt to taste

Soak some trimmed corn husks for several hours in cold water. Next, boil them until they are soft. Remove and dry them thoroughly. Rub the husks with melted lard.

Cut up a fat chicken, cook until very tender in just enough water to cover. Chop up the cooked chicken. Add masa and garlic to boiling hot chicken broth until a thick dough forms. Add salt to taste, anise, and chile pulp. Add 1 T. lard and knead all together until light and smooth. Now to all the chicken pieces add marjoram and enough Chile Sauce No. 1 to mix thickly together. Then add the sliced olives and seedless raisins. Salt to taste and cook together for 5 minutes. Spread the masa evenly over corn husks, about ⅛ inch thick. In the center place 1 large kitchen spoonful of chicken; continue until about 10 are used. Tie ends together with a strip of husk and place on end in a colander over boiling water for 2 or 3 hours.

Variation: Omit the raisins and chile powder or pulp and substitute ¼ C. roasted, de-skinned peanuts and chopped bits of hardboiled egg. Substitute beef for the chicken.

Tamal Budín de Carne
MEAT PUDDING

This recipe requires a pudding bag, for which instructions are given. This recipe uses no garlic, the olives being its substitute. To make a pudding bag, take a piece of scalded, floured muslin cloth. Make a pleat to allow the pudding to expand. Fill the cloth with the mixture and tie securely at the top.

24 Dried Red Chiles
4 Lbs. Brisket of Beef
2 Med. White Onions
Salt

For the Tamal Filling:
2 Lbs. Masa
1 T. Butter
2 Tsp. Baking Powder
1 C. Raisins
1 C. Black Olives

To prepare the chiles, remove the seeds and veins and wash them. Put them into a pot and just cover them with cold water. Bring the chiles to a boil, then remove from the flame. Allow to cool. Drain and reserve the chile liquid. Mash the chiles, adding the chile liquid to make a gravy. Strain this through a colander to remove as much skin as possible.

Boil the meat in a fresh pot of water and when done, allow it to cool. Reserve some of the meat stock for the batter. Next cut the brisket into slices. Put the meat, chopped onion, salt and chile pulp into a large pot and simmer it a few minutes to heat through.

While simmering, make a filling as follows. Combine the masa, butter, and baking powder, mix in enough of the chile and beef stock to make a very stiff batter. Add some raisins and ripe olives. Spread the batter onto a pudding bag, put the meat into the center, tie the bag securely, and boil the pudding in the remaining chile and beef stock. Boil for 2 hours, adding more boiling water as necessary to keep the bag under water.

Tamales de Elotes Verdes
Fresh Corn Tamales

12 Ears of Sweet Corn (white corn on the cob)
1 T. Lard or Butter, softened
Salt

Grate the corn, saving the inner husks. In a food processor, briefly blend the kernels, lard, and salt. Leave the corn as chunky as possible. Spread out a husk and put 1 T. of the mixture on it. Double it over and tie it with a strip of husk. Repeat until desired number is reached. Put some of the grated cobs in the bottom of a large stock pot. Lay the tamales on the cobs, with a plate on top to keep them in place. Add some water, cover the kettle, and steam the tamales for 30 minutes. Serve hot with butter.

Tamales a la Parral
Tamales From the Grape Arbor

4 Lbs. Masa Harina
2 C. lard or Olive Oil
1 C. Beef Broth (or more if needed)
1 Pkg. Yeast
Olive Oil
1½ Lbs. Bottom Round Beef
1 C. Red Chile Pulp
Salt
Pepper
Corn husks

Mix the masa with the lard or olive oil, beef broth and the yeast. Beat well. Set aside to rise for 2 hours or longer. Heat the olive oil in a large skillet and saute the beef until browned. Add the chile pulp, salt, and pepper. Into each corn husk place 2 T. masa and 1 T. meat. Double over, tie, and steam 2 hours.

Tamales al Horno
BAKED TAMALE CASSEROLE

For the Casserole:
2 Lbs. Beef, lean and tender
Water
Salt to taste
Paprika
Corn Meal
8 Oz. Black Olives, minced
15 Oz. Tomatoes (canned), mashed to a purée
Salt
Pepper

For the Sauce:
2 T. Butter
4 T. Flour, browned in non-stick skillet
1 Qt. Water, hot
2 T. Chile Powder
1 Tsp. Salt
2 T. Brown Sugar
1 Lg. Onion, grated
3 T. Vinegar
6 Bay Leaves
¼ C. Sherry
1 Tsp. Oregano
Liquid Hot Sauce (optional)

Cover the meat with water and boil, uncovered, until tender. Remove and reserve liquor. When meat is cool enough, cut into 1 inch cubes. To the stock, add salt and paprika. Add 1 C. cornmeal to 2 C. stock. Lightly boil 30 minutes, adding a little water if necessary. The masa should be spreadable. Into an enameled roaster, put a 2 inch layer of masa. Then add a layer of meat, spread some minced olives over, add a layer of tomato purée, salt, and pepper to taste. Repeat until pan is full, making the top layer the masa dough. Leave a hole in the middle for steam to escape. Bake 45 minutes in a 350 degree oven.

Meanwhile, make the sauce. Melt the butter, add the previously browned flour. Stir this into the quart of water. Add the chile powder, salt, sugar, grated onion, vinegar, bay leaves, sherry and oregano. Boil the sauce well and if not spicy enough, add liquid hot sauce to taste. When the flavors are blended, remove from the fire, let stand to thicken. When ready to serve, reheat and strain. If not thick enough, mix a little sauce and cornstarch, return to the pot and stir to thicken while boiling, lower heat immediately. Pour over each serving of tamale casserole.

Enchiladas No. 1

Enchiladas are what the Californios did with the leftovers. They were never designed to be a meal by themselves. But, that was in the days of the Grandees, when the *almuerzo*, a cross between the American breakfast and brunch, was the big meal of the day. The Mexican verb *enchilar* is composed of *chil*, a diminutive of *chile* and *en*, which means in or upon. The *ar* is the inflected verb ending. Thus, taken as a whole, the word means "a little something in chile."

    1 C.White Onions, finely sliced
    ½ C. Black Olives, chopped
    Olive Oil
    Salt
    4 6-8 inch Wheat Tortillas
    2 C. Chile Sauce No. 1, heated
    1 C. Monterey Jack cheese, grated
    2 Eggs, hard boiled
    ¼ C. Chicken, cooked and chopped
    12 Seedless Raisins, soaked in claret
    Onion, cooked
    Whole Olives

Cook the onions and chopped olives in a little olive oil. In a second skillet, heat olive oil and salt, to almost smoking. Dip each tortilla in it for a few seconds, then dip the tortilla in heated Chile Sauce No. 1. Remove and spread with grated cheese. Put into the center 1 T. cooked onions and olive mix, 1 T. chopped hard-boiled eggs, 2 T. chopped, cooked chicken, 6 seedless raisins soaked in claret, a sprinkle of cheese and a bit of Chile Sauce No. 1. Fold both sides, one over the other and place in a baking pan. Repeat with the remaining tortillas. Pour Chile Sauce No. 1 over all, put 1 T. cooked onion on the center of the top of each and another sprinkling of cheese and 3 whole olives. Place the pan under the broiler and cook till cheese is melted and bubbling. Serve very hot.

Enchiladas No. 2

2 C. Chile Sauce No. 2, heated
2 C. Chicken, cooked and chopped
1 C. White Onion, chopped fine
4 Eggs, coddled or poached
1 C. Monterrey Jack cheese, grated
1 C. Red Chile Sauce No. 1

Use Green Chile Sauce for Enchiladas No. 2. Follow Enchiladas No. 1 recipe for softening them. Fill with chunks of chicken. When folded and ready to put in oven, add onion or coddled or poached egg on top sprinkled with grated cheese. Dribble a spoonful of red chile sauce in spots for color. Run under broiler as above.

❋

Eat Your Hearts Out, Texans

"The original cowboy is a Californian and a nurseling of the adobe, and all his imitations are comparatively feeble."

From Old California Days.

Californians were reputed to be the finest horsemen in the world during the Grandee period. As it was the only means of transportation, and as a typical rancho had from two thousand to five thousand horses available for riding, it seems an easy inference that the following story from San José is probably true: "A caballero wagered that he could, riding at a gallop, pick up a salver of wine glasses with one hand, ride 300 feet to a hotel, and hand the salver and wine glasses to a waiter without spilling a drop of wine. He won the bet."

From Reminiscences of a Ranger.

Many parades in California today reflect the Days of the Dons by featuring fine horses and tackle of the most beautiful workmanship.

❋

Enchiladas Estragón
TARRAGON ENCHILADAS

For the Sauce:
24 Red Chiles (reserve boiling liquid)
2 Lg. Onions, chopped
2 Cloves, Garlic, minced
Butter
2 T. Flour
1 Lg. Tomato, peeled
2 C. Chile liquid
2 T. Tarragon Vinegar or California Salad Vinegar
2 T. Oregano
1 T. *Piloncillo* or Brown Sugar
Salt to taste

For the Tortillas:
4 C. Flour
1 Rounded T. of Lard
1 Tsp. Salt, to taste

For the Filling:
1 Lb. Gouda Cheese, grated
4 C. Green or Ripe Olives
2 Med. Onions, minced
1 Lb. Raisins, soaked in wine or beer
3 Eggs, hard boiled, finely chopped

Split the chiles, remove the seeds, stems and veins, leaving a few veins. Soak the chiles in cold water for 2 hours, change the water, and bring to barely a simmer for 1 hour. Then increase the heat to a boil for 15 minutes. Remove from the flame, set aside to cool. Scrape the pulp with the back of a knife. If the chiles have soaked long enough they will yield ¼ inch of pulp.

Heat a skillet large enough to hold the chopped onions and chile along with the pulp. Sauté the chopped onions and garlic in the butter. Remove the onions and garlic and brown 2 T. flour. Into this put the tomato, onions, garlic, chile purée, and 2 C. of the chile liquid. Season with the tarragon vinegar, oregano, sugar, and salt to taste.

While the chiles are soaking, make the tortillas. Take 4 C. flour, 1 T. lard, and the salt. Mix to coat all the flour with the lard. Moisten with water as for biscuits. Take a ball large enough to roll out a 6 inch diameter tortilla. Roll them out to make a dozen. Stack with wax paper in between tortillas, or they will stick. Bake on a *comal* or un-oiled grill or griddle. Do not let the tortillas brown. Cook one the first side about 1 minute and on the second side about 30 seconds. The tortillas may puff up. This is good. Stack them on a plate in a warm oven.

To make the filling for the enchiladas, have ready the grated Gouda cheese, green or ripe olives, onion, raisins, and hard boiled eggs. Dip the tortilla in the simmering sauce and put on a plate. On one half of the tortilla, put the filling in equal parts, or *al gusto*. Pour 1 T. sauce over the filling and sprinkle 1 T. of the Gouda. Fold to close, pour more sauce over, and sprinkle more cheese. Run under a broiler to slightly melt the cheese. Serve plates piping hot, reminding diners that the plates are hot.

❧

THE OLD FASHIONED WAY TO PREPARE CORN TORTILLAS

Tortillas, like all breads, must be made by feel. No thinking will work, and the manufacturing process must be entirely intuitive. This takes practice, but the results will reward the diner.

Put one gallon of shucked corn in enough water to cover and dissolve one-half cup of slaked lime in a little water and add to the corn. Boil 15 or 20 minutes; remove from fire, pour off the first water and add fresh cold water. Rub by hand to remove the corn silk. Rinse in more water, and it is ready to grind. Don't wash it too much, or it will not be pasty enough to make tortillas.

Grinding had to be done by hand as well. Los Californios would use a metate and mano to do the grinding. Grind the corn into a smooth paste as follows: Three cups corn to one cup of flour, two tablespoons of melted lard, and a teaspoon of salt. Take a piece of dough the size of a biscuit and press it with your hand into a cake the size of small pie plate.

Cook on an ungreased iron griddle or comal. Have ready enough hot salted lard to dip the tortilla in just before you add the filling to make enchiladas.

❧

Enchiladas Americanas
AMERICAN STYLE

1 C. Red Chile Pulp
1 C. Chicken meat, dark
Salt
2 Eggs, beaten lightly
1 C. Milk
½ C. Masa
1 C. Flour
Olive Oil
Parmesan Cheese

Warm the chile pulp. Chop the chicken meat, season with salt and add 2 T. of the purée to it. Beat the eggs, lightly and stir in the milk; add a little salt. Mix the masa and flour. Add the milk into the flour, to make a crêpe batter. Heat olive oil in a non-stick sauté pan. Pour in the batter to make a six inch diameter, thin crêpe. Shake the pan until the mixture is set. Put 2 T. chicken on one side of the tortilla, roll with a knife and remove to a serving dish. When all the crêpes are made, pour the remaining sauce over them and sprinkle with grated parmesan cheese.

WARNING TO MARIACHIS

The earliest guide books to Los Angeles speak of nights around the Plaza as being filled with the cries of tamale vendors in winter and nieves (ice cream) vendors in summer. Another type of cry that was heard around the Plaza caused the following law to be passed during the 1850's. "Ordinance 5. All individuals serenading promiscuously around the street of the city at night without having first obtained permission from the Alcalde (Mayor) will be fined $1.50 for the first offense, $3.00 for the second offense, and for the third, punished according to law." Evidently, with a permit from the Mayor, one was allowed some promiscuous serenading.

Enchiladas de Monica
MONICA'S TASTIEST ENCHILADAS

2 Onions, chopped
Wine Vinegar
Olive Oil
2 C. Chile Sauce No. 1
Vinegar
Sugar
Salt
1 C. Lard or Shortening
12 Corn Tortillas
15 Oz. Ripe Olives
6 Pickles, chopped
1 Lb. Cheese, grated

Prepare the chopped onions by soaking them in wine vinegar for 15 minutes. Heat some olive oil in a pan, add the chile purée and bring to a boil. Add a little vinegar, sugar and salt to taste. Set on a low simmer. Put the lard in a skillet, when hot, fry the tortillas, one by one, for a few seconds to soften. Do not brown them. Put the tortillas on a plate, add the olives, onions, pickle, and cheese in a strip. Roll up immediately. When the dozen tortillas are filled and rolled, drown them in the chile sauce. Garnish with more onions, olives and cheese. Heat in the oven until the cheese melts.

Selling chiles, nuts, rice and beans
Security Pacific Historical Photograph Collection, Los Angeles Public Library

CHAPTER 11

Rice
&
Beans

At the turn of the century, rice, imported from China, made the long, slow ocean crossing and had a long time to dry out during the voyage. It may have required more water for preparation than today's rice varieties, as evidenced by the original versions of some of these recipes, which called for as much as 5 cups of water for each cup of rice. Modern cookbooks call for two cups of liquid to one cup of rice, and this adjustment is reflected in the following recipes.

Always add water or stock that is near boiling. While the occasion is not likely to come up very often, rice cooked over an open wood fire takes on the heavenly fragrance from the wood smoke.

Arroz a la Español Numero Uno
SPANISH RICE NO. 1

From Bertha Ginger comes her secret for perfect rice.

Throw the rice (a spoonful at a time), 1 C. rice to 2 C. water, into boiling hot salted water, boil hard for 10 minutes. Add a pinch of saffron. Then simmer slowly until all the water is absorbed; put an asbestos mat under the vessel and do not stir; grains will be dry and separate from each other.

Arroz Español Numero Dos
SPANISH RICE No. 2

1 T. Bacon, chopped
1 Clove Garlic
1 C. Rice
1 16 Oz. can Tomatoes
1 Tsp. Salt
½ C. Red Chile Pulp
Stock or Hot water

Fry 1 heaping T. chopped bacon, add 1 mashed garlic clove, stir, cook a few minutes. Then add the rice, 1 can of tomatoes, salt, and the cup chile pulp. Cook slowly; when about dry, add meat stock or hot water to finish cooking, but just enough to have rice dry and grains separated when done.

Variation: Along with the garlic, add a chopped medium size onion. Substitute green chile pulp for the red chile pulp.

Arroz con Yerba Buena
SAN FRANCISCO FLAVOR RICE AND MINT

San Francisco's first name was *Yerba Buena*.

2 T. Bacon drippings or oil
1 T. Onion, chopped
½ Tsp. Salt
½ Tsp. Chile Powder
Pinch of Mint Leaves
1 C. Rice
2 C. Hot Water

Heat the bacon drippings, add the onion, salt, chile powder, and mint and slightly cook. Add the rice and stir about until rice begins to color, then add the hot water, cook slowly until all water is absorbed. Pile on platter and cover with Prepared Spanish Sauce.

Variation: Fry some garlic in about 4 ozs. of Chorizo. Add to the above.

Arroz con Queso al Horno

SPANISH RICE AU GRATIN

1 C. Rice
2 C. Water
1 Clove Garlic
1 Tsp. Salt
Chile Sauce No. 1
Grated Cheese

Boil 1 C. rice in 2 C. water, add a clove of garlic, and the salt. When done, remove the garlic. Drain any water and put the rice in a baking vessel; alternate layers of rice, chile sauce, and cheese, ending with the cheese on top. Bake until heated through, and the cheese is a rich brown.

Arroz de Ortega

ORTEGA RICE

The E.C. Ortega Company has been making canned chile, sauces, and other commodities in Southern California since before the turn of the twentieth century. In *Grandma Keeler's Cook Book* is found this recipe calling for Ortega Canned Chile.

1 C. Rice
2 C. Hot water
2 C. Tomatoes, chopped
1 Med. Onion, chopped
5 Ortega's California Peeled Chiles, seeds and veins removed, chopped
½ C. Butter
Salt to taste

Cook the rice in the water about 8 to 10 minutes, until it is half done. Taste a kernel from time to time. When half done, add the tomatoes, onion, chiles, and the butter. Salt to taste. Cook in a double boiler for 4 hours. Check the water level in the boiler every so often.

Arroz con Chiles
GREEN PEPPERS WITH RICE

The lemon and brown sugar lend an authentic Californio touch.

2 T. Red Bell Pepper, chopped
2 T. Green Bell Pepper, chopped
2 T. Onion, chopped
1 T. Salt Pork, chopped
2 C. Tomatoes, chopped
1 T. Chile Powder
½ Tsp. Salt
2 C. Cooked Rice
2 Whole Bell Peppers, stem top cut out, seeded
Butter
Brown Sugar
Lemon

Fry the peppers with the onion with the salt pork until tender. Add the tomato, chile powder, salt, and cooked rice and cook 5 minutes. Fill the peppers with the mixture, put butter on top, sprinkle with brown sugar and lemon juice. Bake in a 350 degree oven 30 minutes.

Arroz con Olivos
RICE WITH BLACK OLIVES

½ C. Olive Oil
1 C. Rice
1 12-Oz. can Black Olives, drained and chopped
2 C. Tomatoes, chopped
2 C. Water
1 Med. Onion, chopped
1 Green Chile, roasted, peeled, seeded, chopped
2 T. Red Bell Pepper, chopped

Heat a pot large enough for the olives, tomatoes, and rice. Add the oil and heat through. Add the rice and keep stirring until it is golden brown. (If you don't watch it, it will scorch, very quickly.) Add the remaining ingredients. Lower the flame and cook until done. Taste a piece of rice every after 15 minutes of cooking and every 5 minutes thereafter to check for doneness.

Arroz con Verduras
HERBED RICE

1 Sm. Veal Knuckle
1 Lg. Carrot
1 Celery Stalk
3 Sprigs Cilantro
1 Bay Laurel Leaf
6 Peppercorns
2 C. Water
½ C. Rice
2 T. Butter
½ C. Tomatoes, strained
1 Med. Onion, chopped
Salt and Pepper to taste

Make a broth of the veal knuckle, carrot, celery, cilantro, bay leaf, pepper-corns and salt with 2 C. water. Boil down to make 1 C. stock. Wash and dry the rice. Brown the rice in butter, then add the tomato and chopped onion. Let cook 2 minutes. Strain the stock over the browned rice and cook over low heat until the broth is absorbed, about 45 minutes.

ETHNIC FOOD DIVERSITY

Chun Chick, a former resident of San Francisco, opened the first Chinese market in Los Angeles in 1861—a combination curiosity shop and grocery store. Also, the influx of Chinese brought about many vegetable truck farms. These "trucks" would be wheeled by the residences, and the truckers would shout out the names of their produce. At one point in time, they all went on strike as prices had fallen precipitously.

Arroz Estofado
STEWED RICE AND PEAS

1 C. Rice
2 C. Water
1 C. lard
3 Garlic Cloves
1 Lg. Onion, minced
1 C. Spring Peas
1 C. New Potatoes, peeled and diced
1 Tsp. Cilantro, minced
4 C. water
2 Avocados, sliced

Boil the rice in the 2 C. water about 15 minutes. Drain immediately into a colander and run under cold water. In a large pot, melt the lard, browning the whole garlic and minced onion. Stir constantly. When brown, remove the garlic. Add the rice, stir constantly to prevent scorching. When the rice is golden brown, pour off the fat, add the peas, potatoes, cilantro, and 4 C. water and simmer for about 1 hour. Pour mixture into rectangular baking dish, garnish with slices of avocado, and serve.

Arroz Arabe
ARABIAN RICE

2 C. Rice
1 C. Butter or Olive Oil
½ C. Onions, minced
2 C. Milk, scalded
1 Clove Garlic, minced
2 C. Chicken stock
1 T. Cilantro, minced
Salt and Pepper to taste

Put butter or oil in an enameled pot to heat. Add the rice and fry until the rice is dry and turns a creamy color. Next, add the onion and garlic, then the hot milk and the chicken stock. Stir in the cilantro, salt, and pepper. Cover, simmer, and let steam until the rice is cooked, 25 minutes.

Arroz con Carne Seca

RICE AND JERKY

While more in the class of a soup or stew, the recipe below, from Ana Bégué de Packman's *Early California Hospitality*, is luscious. She was a descendent of Francisco Sepúlveda, owner of Rancho San Vincente. Back then, it was one of the smaller ranchos, amounting to only 38,000 acres, or about sixty square miles. The area is now the finest part of Los Angeles, comprising Westwood (where UCLA is located), Bel-Air (home to the movie stars), Santa Monica, and the Pacific Palisades (home of the Getty Museum).

2-4 Ozs. Beef Jerky
1 T. Bacon Fat
½ C. Rice
1 Lg. Tomato, chopped
1 Green Chile, roasted, peeled and chopped
1 Med. Onion, peeled and sliced
¼ Tsp. Black pepper
1 Qt. Water

Roast the jerky in a dry cast iron skillet. Heat it just enough to thoroughly soften all of it. Take the meat and pound it until it shreds. In a kettle, heat the bacon fat and fry the rice, tomato, green chile, and onion. Add the black pepper. Next, add the shredded beef. Cover with 1 quart of water and simmer until the rice is done. Taste the rice every so often to check for doneness.

Arroz a la Valenciana
RICE VALENCIANA

The style of ham called for here would be the Asturian ham from Spain. The FDA has strict guidelines for imported hams and The Asturian cannot be found in the United States. Substitute a dry-cured or Smithfield Country Ham.

2 C. Long Grain Rice
2 T. Bacon Fat
1 Sm. Onion, chopped
1 Clove Garlic, chopped
1 C. cold cooked Ham, Chicken, or Veal, minced
Salt and Pepper to taste
1 Tsp. Sugar
5 C. boiling Water

Fry the rice with fat in a skillet until the rice turns a creamy color. Add the onion, garlic, and meat. Season with salt, pepper, and sugar. Add boiling water and simmer uncovered. Do not stir. Serve when rice is done and the grains separate.
Variation: Add a little dry red chile, broken into bits while frying the onion and garlic.

Arroz Azteca
AZTEC RICE

2 C. Milk
1 C. Rice
Salt
3 or 4 Chicken Livers, chopped
1 Can Shrimps, drained
2 Tsp. Curry Powder

In a double boiler, put the milk, rice, and salt. To this add the chicken livers, the can of shrimps, and the curry powder. Allow this to simmer over boiling water until well cooked. Serve on a platter and surround the rice with guacamole.

185

Frijoles
SIMPLE BEANS

Soak the beans overnight. Put in a fresh water in the morning and add ¼ Tsp. baking soda to each quart of water, boil until done, 2 to 3 hours. Boil longer when they are to be mashed. Add salt during the last 30 minutes of cooking.

Salsa de Frijoles
BEAN SAUCE OR DIP

1 C. Kidney Beans
2 T. Olive Oil
¼ C. Onion, chopped
Red or Green Chile to taste
Salt to taste
1-2 T. Flour
Meat Stock

Cook the red kidney beans until they are tender. Put them into a frying pan with hot oil, add onions, green or red chile pulp, and salt, all to taste. Brown a little flour with it, mash beans and press through a sieve or food mill. Add meat stock to thin the sauce. Serve over meat or whole beans.

SPANISH BEANS AU GRATIN

2 C. Cooked Beans
2 T. Lard or Bacon Fat
2 T. Red Chile Pulp
½ C. Monterey Jack or Longhorn Cheese

Put 2 C. well-cooked and drained beans in a large frying pan and add 2 T. hot bacon fat. Add 2 T. red chile pulp and brown. Add ½ C. grated cheese and stir until melted. Sprinkle a little grated cheese on top and run under the broiler to brown.

Variation: The Cacique Company makes a Crema Mexicana. It is similar to a French Crème Fraîche. When the beans are topped with a dollop of it, there is no better eating.

Frijoles Pintos

PINTO BEANS

2 C. Pinto Beans
Water
Salt
Pinch of Baking Soda
1 16 Oz. can of Tomatoes
3 Red Chiles, pulped
3 Green Chiles, pulped
½ C. Onions
2-3 T. Bacon Fat
Salt

Soak beans overnight. Change the water. Boil until tender in salted boiling water with pinch of baking soda. Drain the beans and add 1 can tomatoes, the pulp of 3 red and 3 green chile peppers, and ½ C. onions fried in bacon fat. Salt to taste. Boil slowly until very soft.

Frijoles en Chile Pasilla

BEANS IN FANCY CHILES

4 C. Red Beans
1 Onion, chopped
4 Cloves Garlic
Water
1 C. Beef stock
4 Chile Anchos, stem and seeds removed
8 Chile Pasillas, stem and seeds removed
4 T. Beef Marrow (from the butcher shop)
Salt to taste

Put the beans, the onion, and 4 cloves of garlic in a bean pot. Cover all with water and bring to a boil. Lower flame for a simmering pot and cook, covered all day. Add more water and stir when necessary.

Put the stock in a large enough pot to hold all of the chiles. Put under a slow flame, enough to steam the chiles until they are soft. When they are soft, cool the chiles a little, then scrape the meat from the chiles, discarding the skin. Return the pulp to the steaming water. Put the beef marrow in the stock. When this is boiling hot, return the beans to the stock and heat through. Salt to taste.

SPANISH MASHED BAKED BEANS

2 C. Pinto or Kidney Beans
Water
Salt
Pinch of Baking Soda
Bacon strips to taste
Chile Sauce No. 1
Cilantro

Cook pinto or kidney beans in salted water with pinch of soda until very soft. Drain and mash the beans. Fry the bacon crisp and set aside. Turn the beans into the fat and brown them. Turn out on hot platter. Pour hot Chile Sauce No. 1 over, garnish with bacon strips and cilantro.

Frijoles con Claves
BAKED BEANS MONTERREY

1 Onion
1 Clove
3 Cloves of Garlic
4 Pieces of Mustard Pickle (see recipe)
3 T. Mustard Vinegar (see recipe)
2 C. Red Beans
2 Oz. Salt Pork
Piloncillo or Brown Sugar
Hot Water

In the bottom of a bean pot, put the onion, studded with the clove, the whole garlic, the mustard pickle, and the vinegar. Over this put a layer of uncooked red beans, a piece of salt pork, then more beans. Cover with 1 T. sugar. Carefully fill the pot with boiling water and bake in a 250 degree oven all day or 8 hours minimum. Renew with hot water from time to time.

Variation: Lacking homemade mustard pickle, any non-dill pickle should be somewhat acceptable but the results will suffer a little. Lacking mustard vinegar, use some Dijon-style mustard.

Frijoles de Valle de Santa Maria

SANTA MARIA VALLEY BEANS

2 C. Pink Beans (*pinquintos* if available)
Water
3 T. Olive Oil
2 Cloves Garlic, crushed
½ Can chopped Green Chile
1 Sm. can of Hominy
½ Lb. of Monterey Jack or *Queso Fresco*, diced
1 Sm. can whole Green Chile for each diner
1 Clove per canned chile
Garlic slivers
Salt and Pepper

Cook the beans, covered with water for 2 hours or until they are tender. When ready, remove the beans from the pot, reserving the cooking liquid. In a large skillet, heat 3 T. olive oil, add the garlic and fry it until golden brown. Then add the beans and mash some of them with a spoon to make a little purée. Add the chopped green chile, cheese, and hominy, stir a bit and then add 1½ cups of the reserved bean liquid. Simmer 10 minutes.

Make 2 chiles for each diner. Rub the whole chiles with salt and pepper. Prick the chiles in 2 or 3 places, putting slivers of garlic into them. In one slit, put the clove. Put the chiles in a 300 degree oven for 2 hours. Baste with some of the bean liquor several times. When ready to serve, pour the beans over the chiles and bring to the table in a heated casserole.

Don and Doña early Rose Bowl Parade
Security Pacific Historical Photograph Collection, Los Angeles Public Library

CHAPTER 12

Fillips
&
Finishes

Rajas de Queso Californio
SPANISH CHEESE FINGERS

To serve with all salads.

½ C. Butter
¼ Tsp. Salt
1¼ C. Flour
3 T. Ice Water
¼ C. *Cotija* Cheese, grated (or Parmesan)
2 Chiles *al gusto* (such as minced Serranos)
Cilantro

Make a pie dough with the butter, salt, flour, and ice water. Roll and fold the dough several times. Sprinkle with grated cheese and chile peppers bits or fine slivers. Roll the cheese and slivers into the paste enough to make them stick. Cut the dough in strips, bake in a 400 degree to 425 degree oven, until golden brown. Tie the fingers in bunches with a red ribbon, garnish with a sprig of cilantro.

Pastel Cafe
SPANISH COFFEE CAKE

2 C. *Piloncillo* or Brown Sugar
1 C. Butter
1 C. Buttermilk or regular milk
4 Eggs
3 C. Flour
3 Tsp. Baking Powder
2 Tsp. Cinnamon
Grated *Piloncillo*
Ground Pecans
Cinnamon for garnish

Cream the *piloncillo* with the butter, pour the buttermilk into this. Whip 4 eggs and pour on top of butter and *piloncillo*. Add the flour with 3 Tsp. baking powder sifted through. Next, add 2 Tsp. cinnamon. Mix well and pour into baking tins, sprinkle the top with brown sugar, ground pecans and cinnamon. Bake in medium oven, test with cake pin.

Variation: Add enough flour on rolling board to make a soft dough, cut into large round buns; bake and spread with icing made of hot water and brown sugar cooked until thick with pecan nuts added. Bake in medium oven.

Tortas La Bandera
MEXICAN SANDWICHES

8 Oz. Fresh Red Chiles
8 Oz. Fresh Green Chiles
2 T. Butter for sautéing
Salt to taste
Lemon juice
White and Brown bread (or Tortillas)
Butter
Grated cheese
Cilantro for garnish

If using canned chiles, chop them fine. If using raw, roast, peel and remove the seeds. Next, saute the red and green chiles separately in a little butter, with some salt to taste and a little lemon juice, but don't let the chiles brown. Spread them between layers of thickly cut white and brown bread (or tortillas) alternatively, with the top layer of bread buttered. Layer and sprinkle each thickly with grated cheese. The color effect is pretty when cut in fancy shapes and served on a crisp lettuce leaf.

Variation: Mix red and green chile together. Fry in butter. Allow to cool, add grated cheese, and spread on tortillas that have been dipped in hot butter. Roll lightly, taco style, fasten with a toothpick. Garnish with a sprig of cilantro; serve on crisp lettuce leaves.

❀

BUT DID THEY SERVE FROZEN DAIQUIRIS?

In Los Angeles, two Frenchmen, Damien Marchessault and Prudent Beaudry, opened the first ice house in 1859. Thirty and forty mule-teams hauled wagons loaded with 100-pound blocks of ice from the mountain lakes, fifty miles away. Later, ice was shipped from San Francisco, and when it arrived, the saloons displayed signs soliciting orders.

❀

SPANISH CHOCOLATE CAKE

Get the Mexican chocolate, which is a little round cake about three inches across, with a flavor different from other chocolate.

2 Cakes *Ybarra* or *Abuelita* Chocolate
½ C. Butter
1 C. *Piloncillo* Sugar
4 Eggs
1 C. Milk
3 C. Flour
2 T. Baking Powder
1 Tsp. Vanilla Extract

Icing:
1 Cake *Ybarra* or *Aubulita* Chocolate
1 T. Butter
½ C. *Piloncillo*

Melt 2 cakes of chocolate and add the butter and *piloncillo*. Beat 4 eggs separately, mix the yolks into chocolate, butter, and sugar, beat well. Add the milk, beaten egg whites, flour, baking powder, and vanilla, and stir all together. Bake in a loaf or layers.

To make an icing, take one round of chocolate and melt it with a tablespoon of butter and ½ cup of *piloncillo*. Cook over low heat. When cool, spread on cake or use it as a filling.

Dulce Californiano
CALIFORNIO CANDY

Here are the little thin round cakes which used to be sold on the street 140 years ago around Los Angeles' El Pueblo area.

2 C. *Piloncillo*
½ C. Water
1 Tsp. Butter
Pecans, chopped

Mix the *piloncillo* with the water and butter and cook all together. Place the pecans in the bottom of buttered saucers and pour on sugar-water while it is hot. Let cool.
Variation: Use rum in place of the water.

Arroz con Almendras
ROASTED ALMOND PUDDING

2 C. Rice, uncooked
1 Qt. Milk
4 Egg yolks
½ C. Almonds, roasted and ground
1 C. Sugar
½ Tsp. Salt
½ Tsp. Cinnamon
Pistachio nuts for garnish

Wash the rice well, mix with the milk and allow to stand for 3 hours. Place the rice-milk mixture in a double boiler and cook until the rice is well done, adding more boiling water to the underside of boiler if necessary. Beat the 4 egg yolks. Add to the yolks the almonds, sugar, salt, and cinnamon. Stir into the hot rice-milk and continue to cook 15 minutes. Divide into dessert dishes and set in the refrigerator to cool. When you are ready to serve, sprinkle the top with pistachio nuts.

Camote y Piña
SWEET POTATO AND PINEAPPLE DESSERT

This recipe is still in use in much of Old Mexico, although it is almost unheard of on this side of the border.

1 Lb. Sweet Potatoes
1 Lb. Sugar
½ C. water
½ Pineapple, peeled and grated

Boil the sweet potatoes until tender, peel them, and run them through a food processor. In a stainless steel pan, bring the sugar and water to a candy temperature (225 degrees F.) and add the puréed sweet potatoes. Return to the fire and cook until thick; stirring constantly. Next add the grated pineapple and cook a few minutes longer. Chill and serve in sherbert glasses.

Note on boiling sugar: Use a stainless pot or kettle. Use a candy thermometer. To 1 lb. of sugar add ½ C. water. Put the pot on the heat as for simple syrup. Skim and scrape any froth that forms on the top and sides of the vessel. The sugar will continue to form crystalline grains on the vessel's sides, due to evaporation of the water. Remove them. As soon as the liquid produces small bubbles very close together, the water is completely evaporated. Continuing to heat the sugar will rapidly take it through the various degrees. When all the sugar is 225-230 degrees, it is ready. Remove it from the heat immediately, or it will be ruined, at least for this recipe.

Variation: For extra flavor, use a little *añejo* tequila and dark rum. Add chopped nuts of choice. Brown spices too, may be added: cinnamon, cloves, vanilla extract.

GREAT GRAPES

Mariano de la Luz Verdugo, brought from Loretto (a pueblo in Baja California), the first grape cuttings, which were originally planted by the Padres at the Mission San Diego. Eventually these cuttings supplied all the missions with wine. These became the famous Mission grapes.

Pasas en Vino
WINE AND RAISINS

1 Lb. Raisins
1 C. Red Wine, boiling
2 C. Marsala Wine
Lemon, freshly sliced, thin
Cognac to taste
Fig leaves

Add the raisins to the boiling red wine. When softened, put them in an infusion of Marsala wine, lemon slices and cognac. Let stand 3 days. Next, remove the raisins in bunches the size of a goose egg, wrap in the fig leaves, and bake in a 250 degree oven for 20 to 25 minutes. Send to the table with the leaves cut in the form of an X and turned back so the diners can use a spoon to get at the raisin mixture.

Almendrados
MACAROONS VALLEJO

8 Ozs. Almonds, blanched, skinned, and roasted
8 Ozs. Sugar
3 Ozs. Rice flour
3 Eggs
Almond extract or Vanilla
Almonds, chopped
Coarse Sugar

In the food processor, or mortar, pulverize the almonds. Add the sugar and rice flour and mix well. Beat the white of the eggs very stiff. Put the yolks with the pulverized mixture, mix well. Fold in the whites and stir until creamy. Flavor with almond extract or vanilla. Drop on wax paper, sprinkle with chopped almonds and coarse sugar. Bake in a 350 degree oven 20 minutes, until golden.

Note: Rice flour is readily available at Asian markets around the country.

Mantecado
BUTTER MAKER

This recipe is definitely fiesta fare. Lots of work, but, what results!

1 C. Sugar
1 C. English Walnut meats, chopped
Butter
12 Macaroons (see recipe)

Custard:
2 Eggs
¼ C. Sugar
1 C. Milk
2 Egg Whites, beaten stiff
2 C. Cream
⅓ C. Sugar
Maraschino flavoring

Melt the sugar in a smooth saucepan and add the walnuts. Pour this into a shallow buttered baking dish to harden. Crumble 12 macaroons fine and roast in a dry cast iron skillet.

Make a custard in a double boiler of the yolks of 2 eggs, the sugar, and milk. Pour the custard over the stiff whites and let cool. To the cream add the sugar and beat thoroughly until mixed. Add to this the custard and flavor with maraschino, then freeze. When half frozen, add the macaroon crumbs and half the grated walnut mixture and finish freezing. Sprinkle the remaining walnuts over the frozen cream at serving time.

Torta Frutas
Fruit Torte

The Dough:
3 C. Pastry Flour (otherwise use all-purpose flour)
1 Lb. Butter
1½ Tsp. Salt
1 C. Water

The Fruit:
Pineapple, peeled and sliced
Oranges, peeled and sliced
Bananas, peeled and sliced lengthwise
Lemons, peeled and sliced
Piloncillo or white sugar
Chopped nuts

Mix the dough ingredients and knead for 10 seconds.

Line the sides of a baking dish with the pastry dough. Cover the bottom with slices of pineapple, oranges, banana, and lemon slices. Sift a generous supply of sugar between each layer. Repeat until the dish is full. Cover the top layer with chopped nuts. Bake at 300 degrees for 1 hour or a little longer.

Postre de Manzanas
Apple Dessert

4 Ozs. Blue Cheese
3 Scant T. Butter, room temperature
1 Tsp. Cognac
4 Apples, peeled, cored and thick sliced
Black Coffee in demitasse

Crumble the cheese with a fork and mix thoroughly with the softened butter. Add just enough cognac to well moisten, about 1 tsp. Spread the cheese over the apple slices and serve with coffee in demitasse cups.

Ranfañote

1 C. Molasses
A few Orange peels
½ Tsp. Cinnamon
1 C. American Cheese, crumbled
¼ C. Walnuts, chopped
¼ C. Peanuts, chopped
¼ C. Coconut shreds
¼ C. Dry Bread, broken into bits
2-4 Cloves
½ Stick Butter
Cinnamon to sprinkle

Bring the molasses to a boil with a few orange peels and cinnamon sticks. As it starts to boil, add plenty of crumbled American cheese, chopped walnuts, and peanuts. Add the coconut shreds and the bread, broken up into small pieces, a few cloves, and some butter. Let all come to a boil. Cool on plates and serve sprinkled with cinnamon.

Realengo
ROYAL PATRONAGE FLAN

Fresh fruit of choice, such as Pears, Peaches, Bananas
3 Egg Whites, beaten stiff
¼ Pint Whipping Cream
Sugar, Wine and preserved fruits for decoration

Purée the fresh fruit. Heat and sweeten to taste. Beat 3 egg whites stiff; add gradually to the hot fruit purée, stirring constantly. Butter a mold and turn the fruit into it. Set in a baking dish filled with water and bake in a 300 degree oven until firm. Remove and cover with whipped cream flavored with sugar, wine and preserved cherries.

Atole de Piña
PINEAPPLE DESSERT

    5 pints Water, boiling
    1 Tsp. Salt
    11 Heaping T. Corn Masa
    ½ Lg. Pineapple, grated
    1 Lb. Sugar
    ¼ Tsp. Cinnamon
    1 Pint boiling Water

Into five pints of boiling, salted water, sprinkle the masa. Stir well and boil for 1 hour. Combine the grated pineapple, the sugar, and cinnamon. Add this to a pint of boiling water, stir well, and strain into the boiling masa. Stir well again and pour into custard cups. Serve hot or cold.

Confitura de Piña
DAINTY PINEAPPLE MILK DESSERT

    1 Pineapple, puréed
    6 Pints Milk
    Piloncillo or Sugar to taste
    6 Egg yolks
    6 Ozs. Almonds, pulverized

Peel and core a pineapple. Purée it through a food processor. Sweeten the milk to taste. Beat into it the yolks; strain, and put on the fire. When it has reached a boil, add the almonds and let the mixture cook a few minutes. Next, mix in the pineapple purée and boil until thick. Remove from the fire. It should be thick, but not thick enough to cut into squares, and, therefore, must be eaten with a spoon or fork.

Falta de Bizcocho
California Shortcake

½ C. Butter, softened
1 C. Sugar
3 Eggs, 2 whole, white of 1
⅔ C. Milk, room temperature
2 C. Flour
1 Tsp. Baking Powder
½ Tsp. Cinnamon, ground for cake
1 Tsp. Cinnamon, ground for frosting

Cream the butter and sugar. Beat in the 2 whole eggs till very light, then add the milk and flour with the baking soda and cinnamon sifted into it. Make a thin frosting of the egg white and cinnamon. Frost cake. Put in a 450 degree oven for 20 to 30 minutes, until the shortcake is golden brown. The cinnamon turns the frosting pink.

Puchitas
Shortbread Wafers

½ C. Water
Juice of 1 Lime or ½ Lemon
1 Tsp. Anise seeds
1 T. sugar or honey
1 Tsp. Salt
2 C. Flour
1 Tsp. Baking powder
1 C. Sugar
½ C. Shortening or Beef suet or pork fat
1 Egg, well beaten
Water

Boil the water, lime juice, and anise seeds. Sweeten with sugar or honey. Set the pan aside to cool.

Sift the salt, flour, baking powder, and sugar into a bowl. Mix in the shortening. Stir in the well beaten egg and some water. Knead smooth. Form into marble-sized balls and flatten out with a fork or mold. Bake in a 400 degree oven for 10 to 15 minutes, or until golden brown.

Santa Barbara Panocha

2 Lb. *Piloncillo* or Brown Sugar
1 C. Cream
1 Lb. Pecans, chopped
Buttered wax paper

Boil the sugar with the cream until it forms a thread between the fingers. Remove from the fire and add the nuts. Beat hard until it begins to thicken, then pour on buttered wax paper into round cakes. Allow the cakes to cool and serve.

Flesas con Vino
Strawberries with Marsala

Stem and clean 2 pints of strawberries, dredge in confectioner's or powdered sugar. Put in individual cups or fruit bowl. Sprinkle wine over the berries, let rest 1 hour, and serve very cold. Garnish with mint leaves.

METRIC EQUIVALENTS CHART

Liquid Conversion
1 Teaspoon = 5 Milliliters
1 Tablespoon = 15 Milliliters
¼ Cup = 59 Milliliters
½ Cup = 118 Milliliters
1 Cup = 237 Milliliters
4 Cups = 946 Milliliters
4 Quarts = 3.8 Liters

Dry Conversion
1 Teaspoon = 5 Grams
1 Tablespoon = 15 Grams
¼ Cup = 57 Grams
½ Cup = 114 Grams
1 Cup = 227 Grams

Weight Conversion
1 Ounce = 28 Grams
2 Ounces = 57 Grams
4 Ounces = 114 Grams
8 Ounces = 227 Grams
1 Pound = 454 Grams

SELECTED BIBLIOGRAPHY

Adams, Ramon F. *Come an' Get It; The Story of the Old Cowboy Cook.*
Norman: University of Oklahoma Press, c. 1952.

Aller, Doris. *The Epicure in Mexico, a compilation by Doris Aller of Famous and Fine Mexican Dishes.* [San Francisco]: Colt Press, 1940. Colt Press Epicure Series, No. 3.

Anon. *California Mexican Cook Book.* Los Angeles: E.C. Ortega Company, 1934.

Anon. *The Kirmess Cook Book: 140 Tried Recipes.* Sacramento: H.S. Crocker Co., 1899.

Anon. *Los Angeles Cookery.* Los Angeles: Mirror Printing and Binding House, 1881.

Atkinson, Janet I. *Los Angeles County Historical Directory.*
Jefferson, North Carolina, and London: McFarland & Company, Inc., 1988.

Bancroft, Hubert Howe. *The Works of Hubert Howe Bancroft.* Vol. 35: California Inter Pocula. San Francisco: The History Company, Publishers, 1888.

Bégué de Packman, Ana. *Early California Hospitality.*
Glendale, California: Arthur H. Clark Company, 1938.

Bell, Horace. *On The Old West Coast; Being the Further Reminiscences of a Ranger, Major Horace Bell.* Edited by Lanier Bartlett. New York: William Morrow and Company, 1930.

Belle, Francis P. *California Cook Book; An Unusual Collection of Spanish and Typical California Foods, for Luncheons and Dinners Which May Be Prepared Quickly and Easily.* Chicago: Regan Publishing Corporation, 1925.

Bidwell, John. *In California Before the Gold Rush.*
Los Angeles: Ward Ritchie Press, 1948.

Bryant, Edwin. *What I Saw in California..*
Santa Ana, California: The Fine Arts Press, 1936

Dana, R.H. *Two Years Before The Mast.*
New York: P.F. Collier and Son Corporation, 1937.

Davis, William Heath. *Seventy-Five Years in California, a History of Events and Life in California: Personal, Political and Military; Under the Mexican Regime; During the Quasi-Military Government of the Territory by the United States, and After Admission to the Union.* San Francisco: John Howell, 1929.

Eldredge, Zoeth Skinner. *The Beginnings of San Francisco.*
San Francisco: Zoeth S. Eldredge, 1912

Ginger, Bertha. [Also Bertha Haffner-Ginger and Bertha Palmer]. *The California Mexican-Spanish Cookbook*. Los Angeles: Citizen's Print Shop, 1914.

Jones, Mettie M. Ware, ed. *San Rafael Cook Book*.
San Rafael, California: Melvin & Murgotten Printers, Inc., 1906.

Kappa Alpha Theta. Alumnae Association of Los Angeles. *California Cookery Old & New*. [Los Angeles]: C. Browne, Printer, 1915.

Ladies' Social Circle, Simpson Methodist Episcopal Church, Los Angeles. *How We Cook in Los Angeles; A Practical Cook-Book Containing Six Hundred or More Recipes Selected and Tested by Over Two Hundred Well Known Hostesses, including a French, German and Spanish Department*.
Los Angeles: Commercial Printing House, 1894.

Landmark's Club. *The Landmark's Club Cook Book: A California Collection of the Choicest Recipes from Everywhere, Including a Chapter of the Most Famous Old Californian and Mexican Recipes*. Los Angeles: Out West Co., 1903.

Lindly, Walter, M.D. *California of the South: Its Physical Geography, Climate, Resources*. New York: D. Appleton, 1888.

Linsenmeyer, Helen Walker. *From Fingers to Fingerbowls: A Sprightly History of California Cooking*. San Diego: Union-Tribune Publishing Co., 1972.

Los Angeles Times. *The Times Prize Cook-Book, 453 Good Recipes by California House-Keepers*. Los Angeles: The Times-Mirror Company, c. 1902.

Los Angeles Times. *Los Angeles Times Cook Book No. 2, One Thousand Toothsome Cooking and Other Recipes. Including Seventy-nine Old-Time California, Spanish and Mexican Dishes. Recipes of Famous Pioneer Spanish Settlers*. Los Angeles: The Times-Mirror Company, 1905.

Los Angeles Times. *Los Angeles Times Economy Cook Book No. 5: Practical and Economical Recipes by Skilled Cooks*. Los Angeles: The Times-Mirror Company, 1917.
McClaren, Linnie L. *High Living; Recipes from Southern Climes*. San Francisco: Paul Elder and Company, 1904.

McNeil, Blanche and Edna V. *First Foods of America*.
Los Angeles: Suttonhouse, 1936.

McWilliams, Carey. *Southern California Country; An Island on the Land*.
New York: Duell, Sloan & Pearce, 1946.

Mendez, Anna Maria. *Mexican and Spanish Dishes, To Be Made At Home*.
Los Angeles: Moon Printing, 192-?.

Newman, T. *Grandma Keeler's Housekeeper*.
Los Angeles: Los Angeles Examiner, 1903.

Newmark, Harris. *Sixty Years in Southern California*.
New York: The Knickerbocker Press, 1916.

Out West. Ed. by Lummis, Charles Fletcher. Los Angeles: Land of Sunshine Publishing Co., 1902-1914. Also called *Land of Sunshine*.

Pinedo, Encarnación. *El Cocinero Espanol*.
San Francisco: E.C. Hughes, 1898.

Pitt, Leonard. *Decline of the Californios*.
Berkeley and Los Angeles: University of California Press, 1966.

Queen Ester Circle of the Boyle Heights Methodist Episcopal Church.
Queen Esther Cook Book. Los Angeles: Commercial Printing House, 1904.

Richey, Elinor. *Remain To Be Seen*.
Berkeley, California: Howell-North Books, 1973.

Robinson, Alfred. *Life In California*.
New York: Wiley & Putnam, 1846.

Sanchez, Nellie Van de Grift. *Spanish Arcadia*.
San Francisco: Powell Publishing Company, 1929.

Southworth, May E. *One Hundred & One Mexican Dishes*.
San Francisco: Paul Elder and Company, c. 1906.

Southern California Quarterly.
Los Angeles: Historical Society of Southern California, 1893–.

Taylor, Bayard. *Eldorado; or, Adventures in the Path of Empire*.
Glorieta, New Mexico: Rio Grande Press, 1967.

Tilden, Joe. *Joe Tilden's Recipes for Epicures*.
San Francisco: A.M. Robertson, 1907.

Wiley-Kleeman, Pauline, ed. *Ramona's Spanish-Mexican Cookery: The First Complete Spanish-Mexican Cook Book in English*.
Los Angeles: West Coast Publishing Co., 1929.

Wilson, Iris Higbie. *William Wolfskill: Frontier Trapper to California Ranchero*.
Glendale, California: Arthur H. Clark Company, 1965.

Wise, Henry Augustus. *Los Gringos: or, An Inside view of Mexico and California*.
New York: Baker and Scribner, 1849.

COLOPHON

California Mission Cookery was designed by Lois Bergthold and Deborah Beldring for Border Books of Albuquerque, New Mexico. The Chapter heads were set in 30 point Castellar. The headlines were set in 24 point Galliard and the body text was set in 10 point Galliard.

The book was printed on 55# Natural Windsor Text, by Patterson Printing Company, Benton Harbor, MI.

INDEX